The Blind Musician

The Blind Musician

* * *

Historical, Ophthalmic, Musical, and Neurological Aspects of Gifted Artists

March 2022

Richard H. Fish, MD, FACS

ISBN: 1537396846
ISBN 13: 9781537396842
Library of Congress Control Number: 2016918231
CreateSpace Independent Publishing Platform
North Charleston, South Carolina

Acknowledgments

Special thanks to Jennifer McCarville for academic assistance; Andrew Taylor, associate curator, Visual Resources, Department of Art History, Rice University for assistance with images; Stephen Pflugfelder, MD, M. Bowes Hamill, MD and Ronan O'Malley, MD for proofreading; Olivia Matti for meticulous assistance in the final stages of manuscript preparation; and Jas Obrecht, Natalie Kononenko, and Deirdre O'Connell for proofreading and images related to early blues, Ukrainian minstrelsy, and Blind Tom Wiggins, respectively. Sincere gratitude to Michael Marmor, MD, for starting me on the journey of how visual impairment affects artists and their art.

Finally, I am deeply grateful for the support and funding from Houston Methodist Hospital and its Center for Performing Arts Medicine section.

To the near-blinding lights of my life, Christopher and Allison

Figure 1. Blind harpist. Tomb of Nakht, Thebes, c. 1422–1411 B.C.

Figure 2. *The Blind Fiddler.* Rembrandt van Rijn. Etching, 1631.

Figure 3. *Blind Piper.* Walter Geikie (1795-1837). Print, date unknown.
Image courtesy of Perkins School for the Blind, Watertown, MA.

Figure 4. *The Blind Violinist*, François Grenier De Saint
Martin (1793-1867). Print, date unknown. Image courtesy
of Perkins School for the Blind, Watertown, MA.

Figure 5. *The Blind Piper.* Joseph Patrick Haverty. Oil on canvas, 1841. National Gallery of Ireland.

Figure 6. *The Old Guitarist.* Pablo Picasso. Oil on panel, 1903–04. The Art Institute of Chicago.

Contents

Acknowledgments · v
About the Author · xvii
Foreword · xix
Introduction · xxi

I   "Blindness," Medical Records, Privacy, and Erasure
      by History · 1
II   Sighted versus Blind Musicians and Workarounds · · · · · · · · 3
III   Blind Musicians and Poets in Antiquity · · · · · · · · · · · · · · · 6
IV   The Middle Ages and Renaissance through the
      Early 1800s · 9
V   Blind Composers · 11
VI   Nameless Blind Musicians and Blind Ensembles · · · · · · · · 17
VII   Blind Tom Wiggins (1849–1908) · · · · · · · · · · · · · · · · · · · 23
VIII Blind Blues and Gospel Musicians · · · · · · · · · · · · · · · · · 29
IX   Doc Watson (1923–2012) · 35
X   Art Tatum (1909–1956) · 38
XI   Ray Charles (1930–2004) · 40
XII   Ronnie Milsap (b. 1943) · 43
XIII Jeff Healey (1966–2008) · 45
XIV Andrea Bocelli (b. 1958) · 48
XV   Stevie Wonder (b. 1950) · 52

XVI   Summary of Biographical Material · · · · · · · · · · · · · · · · · 57

XVII Neurological Underpinnings of Blind Musicians and
Cross-Modal Plasticity · 58

XVIII Neuroplasticity with Amblyopia and Its Treatment as
an Example · 62

XIX   Blind Musical Savants, Absolute Pitch, Neuroplasticity,
and Possible Origins of Blind Musical Genius · · · · · · · · · · 64

XX   Further Questions and Conclusions · · · · · · · · · · · · · · · · · · 69

Appendix: Visual Acuity Measurement · · · · · · · · · · · · · · · · 71

Notes · 73

About the Author

Richard H. Fish was born in Houston, Texas and graduated Summa Cum Laude and Phi Beta Kappa from the University of Texas at Austin. He received his medical degree from Baylor College of Medicine in Houston and then completed an ophthalmology residency at the University of Alabama at Birmingham Eye Foundation Hospital and a vitreoretinal fellowship at California Pacific Medical Center in San Francisco. Subsequently, Dr. Fish was an Assistant Professor at the University of Texas Southwestern Medical Center in Dallas for two and a half years prior to moving back to Houston to join Retina Consultants of Houston in 1992. He has lectured extensively and published numerous scientific papers and book chapters on inflammatory and infectious conditions, vitreomacular diseases, and neuro-ophthalmologic disorders. He is a nationally recognized specialist in the research and treatment of opportunistic infections of the eye and is a scientific reviewer for two major ophthalmic journals.

Dr. Fish is a Clinical Associate Professor at Baylor College of Medicine and Weill Cornell Medical College, a member of the American Society of Retina Specialists, a Fellow of the American College of Surgeons, and a past President of the Houston Ophthalmological Society. At Houston Methodist Hospital, he is the former Deputy Chairman of the Department of Ophthalmology and a physician member of the Center for Performing Arts Medicine (CPAM), lecturing regularly on "Eye

Diseases of Visual Artists" and "Blind Musicians." In his spare time Dr. Fish is an active world traveler, an avid photographer, and a semi-professional musician. He plays drums in the University of Texas Longhorn Alumni Band, two rock and roll bands comprised of doctors, and in two jazz bands.

Foreword

I have been an enthusiastic musician since the age of eight: marching and concert bands throughout high school and college, jazz and rock-and-roll bands intermittently. During the long years of medical training—medical school, residency in ophthalmology, fellowship in vitreoretinal surgery—and for my first decade of academic and then private practice, playing drums and guitar became less important than raising a family. In 2003, much to my delight, I was asked to join a rock-and-roll band as the drummer. Another rock-and-roll band asked me, then a jazz band, and then another, and music and gigging became, once again, a tremendously important and gratifying part of my life. At the age of fifty, I lost all hearing in my left ear (not related to loud music or drumming).

Contemporaneous with my struggle as a slightly disabled musician, I became interested in visual impairment in painters through Mike Marmor and James Levin's marvelous pair of books *The Eye of the Artist* and *The Artist's Eyes*. One a textbook and the other more geared toward a lay readership, these books comprehensively cover the fascinating history of Claude Monet's cataracts and Edgar Degas's visual impairment. Mary Cassatt, Georgia O'Keeffe, Edvard Munch, Camille Pissarro, and James Thurber all had some form of ophthalmic disease or visual impairment and these artists, as well as other topics related to art and artists' visual perception are covered magnificently in these two books. Eventually, that led me to a tangential and equally intriguing topic that started with two simple questions: What is so special about blind musicians, and why are there so many prominent and talented ones throughout history?

These questions led me to compulsively read every biography and autobiography of every prominent blind musician and delve into the archives regarding ancient blind poets, minstrels, and musicians across cultures and throughout history. I became absorbed by the ophthalmic and medical literature on auditory processing in blind individuals, neuroplasticity, and gifted musical savant syndrome. My goal is to present, as a single source, a review on the subject of blind musicians, including ophthalmic diagnoses and treatments of these musicians, fascinating historical vignettes, and the musical significance of each artist. Moreover, I have attempted to summarize some complicated medical literature on the neurological underpinnings of this extraordinary musical ability. I have attempted to cover what I felt to be the most important or personally fascinating biographies and the most relevant science. I wanted this to be a comprehensive, not necessarily an exhaustive, review. I hope that curious readers will have their interest piqued and read some of the wonderful primary source material referenced and also listen to some of the compositions and contributions of these amazing artists. It is to these gifted individuals, who to a person would never describe themselves as disabled, that this book is dedicated.

Introduction

Music was made for blind people.

—Jacques Lusseryan, blind writer, cellist, and
hero of the French Resistance[1]

Outside the circle of those who care about or care for them, blind individuals have usually been met with reactions ranging from curiosity to revulsion. Depending on the society or era, blind persons were traditionally thought to have been somehow deserving of their affliction, punished by gods, demons, or enemies for some transgression (e.g., Oedipus, Samson);[2] itinerant beggars, placed on the lowest rungs of the social ladder because of sin and moral failure;[3] or supernaturally gifted with insight (e.g., Tiresias, the blind prophet of Greek mythology).[4] The blind musician, on the other hand, has been almost universally esteemed, and the association of extraordinary musical skills and blindness exists across many cultures throughout history.[5] [6] [7] As Terry Rowden, writing in the introduction of his superb book, *The Songs of Blind Folk: African American Musicians and the Cultures of Blindness*, states, "No role has been more strongly linked to disability than musicianship has to blindness. The idea of the special aptitude of blind people for music has all but been taken for granted."[8] Blind musicians have been etched into many cultures, reflected in their frequent use as subject matter for visual artists across centuries (Figs. 1–6).

In this review, we explore the fascinating biographies of a number of blind musicians, composers, and ensembles, commenting on their musical significance and offering some suggested works. We will also delve into their ophthalmic histories, diseases, and treatments when known. We will review the possible neuroanatomic and neurofunctional underpinnings of increased musical ability, requiring an exploration of blind musical savants. Finally, discussions of neuroplasticity will be offered as possible etiologic pathways to the development of these extraordinary musical skills.

I

"Blindness," Medical Records, Privacy, and Erasure by History

In the lay literature and all source material cited, including every artist biography and autobiography, "blindness" is stated as fact. There is, however, no attempt made to grade the extent of vision loss: terms like *hand motions* or *bare light perception* make no appearance in these documents (see appendix). Moreover, even a rudimentary distinction among total blindness, legal blindness, and functional blindness [9] is usually not explicitly conveyed (but can occasionally be estimated or inferred). Except when noted, we will assume that the musicians profiled were at best not able to see their musical instruments or music and were at worst (and more likely) without light perception, phthisical,* or surgically anophthalmic† due to an end-stage disease process.

Similarly, biographical and autobiographical material of interest to the general public usually has devoted very little to the precise etiology of the blinding disease. This might be attributable to the artists' near-uniform desire to de-emphasize their blindness; to be considered serious musicians, composers, or performers; or to mainstream into their broader societies. Most of the artists were either congenitally blind (CB) or early blind (EB), and many were born into and lived in extreme

---

* Phthisis bulbi is the condition in which an eye, usually through severe disease or trauma, becomes shrunken and nonfunctional.

† Anophthalmos (Gr., "without eye") is the absence of an eye, either congenitally or as the result of surgical removal of the globe.

poverty with limited medical care. The eras in which these musicians were treated for blinding conditions range from decades ago to centuries ago. Examination techniques can be presumed to have been limited or nonexistent, and absolutely no medical records are available for scholarly study. Accordingly, we have only limited data to study the medical or ophthalmic histories of these musicians, and there are likely many inaccuracies that have been relayed to the musician himself (interestingly, very few blind women musicians have achieved prominence) and have been passed forward to biographers. Nonetheless, we will attempt to comment on the ophthalmic histories, inexact as they may be, as they are commonly understood.

II

Sighted versus Blind Musicians and Workarounds

Most sighted musicians learn musical notation and its rules and develop an understanding of music from visual—the ability to read music from a page—as well as auditory input. One skill in particular tied to vision is the ability to immediately read and play an unfamiliar piece of music—sight reading. Sighted ensemble instrumentalists or vocalists learn and benefit from the visual cues from the teacher or the conductor. It is self-evident that blind musicians are compelled to learn their instrument or instruments in the absence of any musical notation and without the benefit of a conductor, using auditory and tactile rather than any visual modalities.[10] In contrast, every piece by a blind musician has relied on nonvisual composition, transcription by another person or by a computer, and total memorization during performance. Likewise, as performers, blind musicians have to use non-visual modalities to interpret and control their audiences' reactions, which may in part determine their success or popularity.[11]

Nonetheless, many blind musicians have found workarounds and acquire tremendous skill instrumentally and/or vocally, achieving great popularity. By virtue of their oral rather than written transmission, some forms of music lend themselves to playing in the absence of musical notation or a conductor, notably blues and jazz,[12] and a disproportionate number of the artists profiled here achieved their success in those genres. In addition, there is a well-established method for musical notation for the blind. Louis Braille, who was blinded at age three by a traumatic injury and subsequent sympathetic ophthalmia,[*][13] became an accomplished organist[14] and created his tactile reading system for musical notation. The same two-by-six cells of raised dots that are universally used to represent the alphanumeric system are also arranged in a different manner to notate pitch, sharps or flats, octave position, duration, and articulation of musical notes (Fig. 7).[15]

---

* An extremely rare condition in which trauma to one eye (the "inciting" eye) causes severe, potentially blinding inflammation in the fellow ("sympathizing") eye.

Figure 7. Examples of Braille musical notation. From De Garmo, MT. *Introduction to Braille Music Transcription, 2nd Edition.* National Library Service for the Blind and Physically Handicapped. Library of Congress, 2005. Reprinted with permission.

III

Blind Musicians and Poets in Antiquity

As far back as the second millennium B.C., references to blind court minstrels or blind singers are found in ancient China[16] and on Egyptian tomb paintings. (Fig 1).[17] The infirmity of blindness appears frequently in ancient Greek writings, usually associated with either the gift of prophecy or poetry. Some of the earliest blind musicians were the ancient Greek epic poets, reciting the cycles of the hero while accompanying themselves on the lyre.[18] [19] Setting aside the long-debated Homeric Question (exactly when, how, and by whom the Homeric poems were written),[20] the most famous blind figure from this period is Homer himself (c. 1100–c. 800 BC). By literary tradition, Homer's blindness has been described since at least the fifth century BC, and in the visual arts, he is almost universally depicted as a blind, wise old man (Fig. 8).[21] [22] In fact, despite what little is known of Homer in other aspects of his life and writings, one of the remarkably stable features of his persona is his blindness.[23] The blind poet Demodocus, who has been interpreted by both ancient and modern readers to be an autobiographical figure,[24] [25] is introduced in *The Odyssey*:

> The herald came near leading the faithful singer. The Muse loved him exceedingly, and gave him a good gift and a bad one: she deprived him of his eyes, but gave him sweet song.[26]

Figure 8. Bust of Homer, Epimedes type. Marble, Roman copy of Greek original from fifth century BC. Museo Pio-Clementino, Vatican City.

One scholar interprets this passage to signify that "blindness and song are 'contemporaneous' attributes: neither precedes the other, both are basic to the singer's character."[27] Another supports the notion that Homer might also have been a singer, "depending on the context...of the text in question, Homer is represented as a singer or as a poet." [28]

IV

The Middle Ages and Renaissance through the Early 1800s

Francesco Landini (c. 1325–1397) was a preeminent composer of vocal, choral, and string pieces in fourteenth-century Florence. Blinded by small-pox as a child, he became a master organist and was referred to as "Master Franciscus, Blind Organist of Florence" or "The Blind Man of Florence." In the late medieval period, musical composition was generally not notated; instead, musicians relied on memory and interaction with vocal or instrumental improvisation. Landini was famous for both his prodigious memory and his improvisatory skill, both of which were noted by his contemporaries to have been enhanced by his blindness.[29] Other notable blind musicians of this era include the Nuremberg organist Conrad Paumann (1410–1473), a leading figure in German instrumental music; Antonio de Cabezón (1510–1566), an organist and harpsichordist to King Charles V and Philip II of Spain; and Arnolt Schlick (d. after 1527), a Heidelberg organist, lute player, and influential composer of organ pieces.[30]

"Blind Harry" or "Henry the Minstrel" (c. 1140–c. 1493) was, by tradition, a wandering minstrel, a poet, and the author of the twelve-volume, 11,877-stanza epic poem "The Wallace." The original *Blind Harry's Wallace*, written circa 1477 and translated and adapted in 1722 by William Hamilton of Gilbertfield, recounts the history of William Wallace, who lived, led the movement for Scottish independence, and died a century or more before the poem was published.[31] [32] More recently, William Wallace was depicted in the Academy Award winning film *Braveheart*.

Second to the Bible, *Blind Harry's Wallace* became the most popular work of literature of all time in Scotland.[33] Blind Harry was well known and respected in his time, yet information on him is sparse. There are court records of payments made to him for singing his compositions to the king and nobility between 1473 and 1492.[34] But similarly to Homer, Blind Harry is the subject of vigorous academic debate as to whether or not he was actually blind; whether he did or could have written the epic poem if he were blind, since none of the memory-aiding meters of Greek epic poetry are present in his work; and how historically accurate or embellished was his treatment of his subject.[35] [36]

Blindness was common among Celtic harpers (the preferred term for harpists in this genre of music) and pipers.[37] [38] A tradition of teaching blind boys to be musicians was shared by Scotland and Ireland (Fig. 5).[39] The word *dall* (Gaelic or Celtic for *blind*) was frequently added to the names of these musicians, notably Dall O'Cathan; Ruairidh Dall Morrison; and Iain Dall ("Blind John") MacKay, "The Blind Piper of Gairloch."[40] [41] [42] In many of these cases, blindness was due to smallpox (variola).[43] In the post-eradication era, with the last naturally occurring case of smallpox recorded in Somalia in 1977,[44] it is worth recalling the devastating ocular complications of smallpox. The majority of references in a 2003 review were from the late 1800s to the 1920s and included cases of severe blepharoconjunctivitis* with or without pustules, keratitis, corneal ulceration with perforation and the sequelae of perforation, bacterial superinfection, disciform keratitis,† corneal scarring with eventual leukoma,‡ iritis, retinitis, and optic neuritis.§ [45]

---

* Inflammation and/or infection of the eyelid and conjunctiva, the thin membrane that covers the eye.

† Inflammation or infection of the cornea—the clear window through which light passes—which results in a disc-shaped area of inflammation and scarring.

‡ A dense, white corneal opacity, usually the result of scarring from inflammation or infection, preventing any view of the iris.

§ Inflammation or infection of the iris, retina, or optic nerve, respectively.

V

Blind Composers

All sighted musical composers use written or other media to notate their compositions. The disability of Ludwig van Beethoven (1770–1827), whose hearing loss began at age twenty-eight leading to total deafness by age fifty, is well known and will not be covered here except to illustrate that he and other deaf composers were able to work and transcribe music without auditory function presumably by "hearing" the music internally.[46] [47] In contrast, a blind composer has limited to no ability to use conventional written musical notation. Technological advances from Braille musical notation to tape recording to computer software specifically for composition[48] and, most importantly, the advent of MIDI (musical instrument digital interface) instruments and software[49] have rendered these limitations mostly obsolete. Prior to these developments, a blind composer would have to hire an *amanuensis*, an assistant who could transcribe the composer's playing into written manuscripts. John Stanley (1713–1786) was an early blind composer, a contemporary of Handel who was held in high regard by the master and used an amanuensis for composing.[50] [51]

In his later years, George Frederick Handel (1685–1759) also employed an amanuensis, his friend John Christopher Smith.[52] Handel's musical heritage is indisputably rich and extensive, his deteriorating visual acuity and its treatment largely a historical and medical mystery. Handel was born to German parents, moved to London in 1712, and became a naturalized British subject in 1727; he is considered one of the greatest and most prolific of the British composers, helping to transition baroque music away from Italian opera to what he is most remembered for—the English oratorio.[53] Most known for his compositions "Music for the Royal Fireworks," "The Water Music," and "The Messiah," Handel wrote forty-two operas, twenty-nine oratorios, more than one hundred twenty cantatas, duets, trios, sonatas, Italian arias, chamber music, Latin church music, anthems, concerti grossi, and numerous orchestral and keyboard works.[54] His compositional output equals almost all of those of Bach and Beethoven combined, but the public preference for just one ("The Messiah") has led to most of this great output remaining unfamiliar.[55]

Previous work by Blanchard[56] has summarized what is known about Handel's blindness late in his life. Briefly, at the age of sixty-six, Handel lost vision in his left eye. He departed London to take the waters at Bath and Cheltenham, then returned to consult with Samuel Sharp at Guy's Hospital who made the diagnosis of *gutta serena*, a "condition of severe visual acuity loss not favorable to surgery"[57] or blindness with no external signs of disease.[58] [59] Despite poor vision, which had now affected his right eye also, he finished and presented the first performance of his oratorio "Jephtha" in 1752. In November of 1752, he underwent a couching* procedure by William Bromfield, the Princess of Wales's surgeon.[60] His vision continued to deteriorate, and by March of 1753, he was completely blind. He continued to perform and became known for his "inventive powers" of mostly memorized or extemporaneous organ pieces.[61]

At this point the story gets murkier. Most of the biographies of Handel report that a final, desperate attempt was made to save his vision

---

* An outdated procedure for treating a cataract in which, instead of removing the cloudy lens (cataract), the lens is surgically dislocated into the back part of the eye, clearing the obstruction to vision. It is an archaic form of cataract surgery, dating back to ancient Egypt, but was still performed as late as the 1800s. The complication rate and dismal outcomes led to development of safer and more effective techniques by the early twentieth century through the current era.

by consulting with John Taylor Sr. (1703–1772), who performed additional surgery, possibly another couching procedure.[62] [63] [64] Taylor has been profiled in several publications, notably by Albert and Henkind,[65] but Lang has perhaps the most succinct and colorful description of Taylor:

> an eye specialist also known as "the Chevalier." This "ophtalmieter" was a quack, though eventually boasting the title of court oculist to George III. If the operation really took place (Taylor's memoirs are filled with unreliable and inaccurate stories), this suave adventurer can claim to have contributed substantially to the misery of the two greatest musicians of the age. It was Taylor who in 1750 operated on the blind Bach—equally unsuccessfully.[66]

There is quite a bit known about the "Chevalier" Taylor. He coined the now-extinct term *ophthalmieter* (Greek for *eye* and *physician*) and was one of the first to concentrate on diseases of the eye. He traveled throughout Europe, demanding exorbitant fees and threatening those who did not pay with lawsuits. He advertised his arrival, entered a city with two coaches and servants in livery, and operated with golden instruments. He operated on Johann Sebastian Bach in Leipzig in 1750. The surgery was unsuccessful, necessitating a second surgery shortly thereafter and drastic postoperative care, including incisions, poultices, mercury compounds, and bleeding. A weakened Bach died in the same year that he was treated by Taylor.[67] Albert and Henkind[68] and one of Handel's most prominent biographers, Christopher Hogwood,[69] acknowledge that the evidence of Taylor's having operated on George Frederick Handel is scanty, apart from Taylor's self-effusive claims. The precise etiology of Handel's blindness is another unknown. Blanchard hypothesized the most likely condition that would have caused severe loss of vision in both eyes in an elderly, overweight male (Fig. 9) as nonarteritic ischemic optic neuropathy,* and "Handel easily fits into the criteria for diagnosis of this disease."[70]

---

* Essentially, a "stroke" of the optic nerve in which the blood supply to the optic nerve is compromised, resulting in damage to the nerve and loss of vision. More common in persons with obesity, diabetes mellitus, and hypertension.

Figure 9. Portrait of George Frideric Handel. William Bromley, after Thomas Hudson. Line engraving published 1786, National Portrait Gallery, London.

Two other blind composers are worth attention. Frederick Delius (1862–1934) was an English composer who contracted syphilis while living in France. Tertiary syphilis eventually left him with upper extremity paralysis and blindness. A young musician, Eric Fenby, was hired as his amanuensis, which permitted Delius to resume composing. Delius's blindness later in his life left critics of his time divided as to whether his post-blindness music represented a "triumph over disability (or was)... marred by disability."[71] Notable works by Delius include "On Hearing the First Cuckoo in Spring," "The Walk to the Paradise Garden," "Summer Night on the River," and "Songs of Farewell."

Joaquín Rodrigo (1901–1999) is perhaps Spain's best-known and most beloved composer. Born in Sagunto, in the Valencia province, he contracted diphtheria in an epidemic of 1905. He was left virtually blind,[72] although "he could still see light and colors."[73] At the age of four, his parents took him to Barcelona, where Dr. Ignacio Barraquer—the patriarch of the ophthalmic Barraquer family—operated on young Joaquín, resulting in bare light perception vision.[74] His best-known work, "Concierto de Aranjuez," with its stirring and instantly recognizable second movement, was composed, like his other works, using Braille musical notation.[75] As was the case with smallpox, it is worth reviewing the ocular manifestations of the rarely encountered disease that purportedly blinded Rodrigo, noting that the references to ophthalmic manifestations of diphtheria date to as far back as the mid–1800s. These include membranous or pseudo-membranous conjunctivitis; ecchymotic and boardlike lids; conjunctival scarring with xerosis, symblepharon, trichiasis, and entropion; and corneal ulceration.[*] [76] [77] [78] Neither the particular manifestations of ocular diphtheria that Rodrigo suffered from nor what surgery

---

[*] Ecchymosis: medical terminology for bruise—a discoloration of the skin due to collection of blood within the skin; xerosis: extremely dry skin or, in this case, conjunctiva; symblepharon: adhesions of the conjunctiva from the eyelid to the globe, usually the result of infection; trichiasis: ingrowth of eyelashes toward, instead of away from, the eye; entropion: turning of the eyelid inward, usually due to infection or inflammation, causing discomfort due to lashes rubbing the eye.

Barraquer might have performed in 1905 are known. It is unlikely that full-thickness corneal transplantation* was done, as the first reported case was published in 1906.[79]

---

* Corneal transplantation is the removal of the scarred or diseased cornea and replacement with a clear, healthy donor cornea. The cornea was one of the first human tissues successfully transplanted, and corneal transplantation remains among the transplant procedures with the highest success rates in all of medicine.

VI

Nameless Blind Musicians and Blind Ensembles

Despite their affliction, numerous blind individuals have found fulfill-ment and employment through music. Blindness throughout history has been closely associated with poverty and music one of the few respect-able careers available for the blind.[80] In some instances, however, blind persons were specifically recruited into the musical profession or into a musical ensemble.

Blind professional cantors (*mu'allimūn*) (Fig. 10) have been used for centuries in the Coptic church, with traditions and hymns inher-ited from their ancient Egyptian ancestors.[81] Coptic liturgical chants are elaborate, melodious hymns that can take up to twenty minutes to sing and sometimes require pages of music for a single syllable. Many of these hymns have been too complex to be transcribed onto paper. Consequently, the music has been committed to memory and handed down orally for nearly twenty centuries by the blind cantors.[82][83] In 1893, chanting was taught at the newly formed Saint Didymus Institute for the Blind at the Coptic Theological Seminary. A Braille system for the Arabic and Coptic alphabets was established, aiding the blind *mu'allimūn*. While some blind Coptic cantors still exist, most have been replaced by recordings or sighted singers.[84]

Figure 10. Blind Master Coptic Cantor Mikhail al-Batanouni (1873–1957). Photograph courtesy of Laurence Moftah. Reprinted with photographer's permission from *A Musical Inheritance: Coptic Cantors and an Orally Transmitted Tradition*, Library of Congress.

Another fascinating chapter in the annals of blind musicians—blind Ukrainian minstrels who had their peak in the period from 1850-1939—has been expertly chronicled by Kononenko.[85] Minstrels were either *kobzari*, who played a string instrument similar to the lute, or *lirnyky*, minstrels who played an instrument similar to a crank-driven hurdy-gurdy (Fig. 11). Although the minstrels probably date to well before the nineteenth century, their repertoire of religious stories, historical epics, and specific begging songs (*zhebranka*) probably dates to the fourteenth century.

In a rural, agrarian country with high poverty and limited access to medical care, cases of smallpox, measles, diphtheria, scarlet fever, and trachoma were common, resulting in a disproportionately high number of blind children. Secret guilds were formed to administer the three- to six-year apprenticeship of blind children, which usually started by age ten or twelve. Blindness, not musical aptitude or talent, was the sole criterion for entry into the guilds and absolutely obligatory to minstrelsy in Ukraine. Since every family member was expected to work, and agricultural work would be impossible for the blind, minstrelsy developed into an effective social welfare institution, assuring that the blind would not be a burden on their communities.[86]

Although hard academic evidence is scarce, the story of the diminution of the minstrels—perhaps apocryphal—is also fascinating. Threatened by the nationalistic art of the minstrels, Joseph Stalin considered the *kobzari* and the guilds to be counterrevolutionary. In 1939, he called a convention in Kharkiv patterned on previous festivals and drew minstrels from the numerous small villages of Ukraine, ostensibly to celebrate their talent and history. Upon the conclusion of the festival, the men were purportedly gunned down and exterminated.[87] [88] In recent years, the music and traditions of the Ukrainian minstrels have been resurrected, with musicians receiving conservatory training and no longer required to be blind.[89]

Fig 11. Blind Ukrainian minstrels, consisting of *kobzari* and *lirnyky*, c. 1926. Notice the children (seated), presumably minstrels' guides (*povodyri*). Photograph courtesy of Natalie Kononenko, from the collection of Ivan Honchar.

The Al-Nour Wal Amal (*Light and Hope*) Chamber Orchestra (Fig. 12) consists entirely of forty-four blind female musicians between twenty and forty years of age. Sometimes referred to as the Blind Orchestra of Cairo, the chamber orchestra (by definition, usually fifty or fewer musicians) is an offshoot of the Egyptian Blind Girls Association, founded in 1954. The school has a dormitory and occupational training and in 1961 added music education. As youngsters, girls are tested for musical aptitude. They choose instruments and learn Braille musical notation. A junior orchestra of younger students feeds the main orchestra with young women. Almost all of the women are Muslim.[90] [91] Their repertoire consists of Western classical music, works by Egyptian composers, and orchestral versions of Egyptian music. The players commit all music to memory and rehearse with a music director, who coaches the ensemble with verbal instructions. The orchestra has performed worldwide and is the only orchestra in the world that can see neither its music nor its conductor. Nonetheless, it is noted for its ability to gradually shift tempo and dynamics, skills for which the ability to see and follow a conductor's cues would ordinarily be crucial. In his book *Music, Disability, and Society*, Alex Lubet's admiration for the orchestra is tangible:

> That its membership consists of girls and women in a mostly Muslim Arab country—where there is considerable circumspection regarding music, women in public life, and Western culture, and where blind girls are afforded few opportunities for... growth...the almost half century flourishing of this ensemble is all the more transgressive and liberatory.[92]

Unfortunately, political, economic, and security concerns have threatened the orchestra since the January 2011 Egyptian revolution.[93]

Having reviewed blind epic poets, minstrels, composers, and ensembles, with significant attention to distant history, we now turn to

Figure 12. Al-Nour Wal Amal Orchestra. Photograph by Fernando Moleres.

individual blind musicians whose appearances in recent history create a larger pool of information from which to draw. Here at least the historical and musical records are more accessible, even if the same problem of incomplete or inaccurate ophthalmic histories is still present.

VII

Blind Tom Wiggins (1849–1908)

Deirdre O'Connell has written a comprehensive and engrossing biography [94] of Blind Tom Wiggins (sometimes Bethune, as slaves were sometimes known by their master's family names) but his story is so fascinating that it is worthy of significant attention here. Tom Wiggins was born blind—cause unknown—in Columbus, Georgia. A blind child, in terms of labor value, was considered worthless. Accordingly, few disabled children born into slavery survived—the infant would be euthanized and become another death in an age of high infant mortality.[95] Tom's first master indeed wanted him dead,[96] so at the age of eight months, Tom was sold as an "add-on" to the purchase of his parents by General James Bethune.[97] Most accounts reveal that Tom may not have been completely blind, perhaps with the ability to differentiate light from dark, but was almost certainly without functional vision.[98] As he grew up on the Bethune farm, he developed total recall for and phenomenal vocal mimicry of every-day sounds and noises. [99] He had minimal but at least conversational language skills[100] but demonstrated echolalia.* These attributes have led most contemporary biographers and scholars to conclude that Tom had early infantile autism.[101] His autism, however, was filtered

---

* Meaningless repetition of another person's words, usually the result of a mental or psychiatric condition.

by the prevailing racial attitudes of the time, allegedly demonstrating incontrovertible proof of the innate musical gifts but natural inferiority of the Africans to Europeans.[102]

In 1853, the Bethunes purchased a piano. Barred from entering the house, Tom took up unofficial residency outside the parlor window or directly under the piano beneath the house. The Bethunes embellished the story over the years, but common to the many accounts is that at some point, with no prompting or instruction, a four-year-old Tom, having heard one of the Bethune girls playing a melody earlier in the day, began to play the piano so proficiently that, given his age and disability, it seemed practically supernatural.[103] [104]

As O'Connell writes, "perhaps the watershed...was not Tom's discovery of the piano, but General Bethune's discovery of Tom."[105] Tom was moved into the main house, began playing the piano with an all-consuming passion, and musically imitated the sounds he heard from nature, weaponry, and trains. His first composition at the age of five, "Rain Storms," beautifully mimics clouds and rain rolling in, thunder, and turmoil before returning to its melodic opening theme. By the time Tom was eight, Bethune had licensed him to a Barnum-style showman who promoted him as "Blind Tom" (Fig. 13), the stage name by which he would forever be known. His concerts were a mix of energetic playing, imitative pieces, and suggestions by his manager that he was "channeling the great masters" as if in a séance. Tom had absolute pitch,[106] [107] and a phenomenal musical memory—it was claimed that he had a repertoire of more than five thousand pieces. He was able to play two unrelated works simultaneously, one with each hand (e.g., "Yankee Doodle" and "Dixie"), even with his back turned to the piano.[108] [109] Part of his appeal was the incongruity of beautiful, highly cultivated music emanating from a monstrous, uncivilized body.[110] Looking back at the evidence available from texts, newspapers, and periodicals of the time, it has been concluded that Tom was a blind musical savant.[111]

Fig. 13. Advertisement for Blind Tom Wiggins performance, 1868. Image courtesy of Deirdre O'Connell.

In June 1860, Tom made his Washington, DC, debut. President James Buchanan's niece Harriet Lane—by default America's first lady, as Buchanan was the only US bachelor president—heard him play. This led to an invitation to play for the president, and at the age of ten, Tom became the first African-American performer to play at the White House.[112] [113] During his Washington trip, Tom listened to debates in Congress, filled with epithets, pejoratives, and denunciations of both Abraham Lincoln and Stephen Douglas and subsequently began to imitate the speeches word for word, complete with the scandalous language, to a rousing response from his audiences. He was especially adept at imitating Douglas's speeches, including Douglas's vocal inflections and the catcalls that Tom had heard from the crowds.[114]

During the Civil War, Tom's performances were confined to Southern states. His management donated unknown (but reportedly large) amounts of the proceeds from Tom's concerts to the Confederate war effort. After one of the early Confederate victories, Tom composed and would subsequently play at every concert what would become his most well-known piece, "The Battle of Manassas." Containing excerpts from "Dixie," "Yankee Doodle," "The Star Spangled Banner," and "La Marseillaise," as well as piano imitations of musketry, artillery, soldiers marching, and galloping horses, "The Battle of Manassas" shows remarkable creativity and musicality and was quite popular at the time due to its sonic recreation of one of the South's greatest victories.[115]

As the end of the Civil War approached, legal battles began over Tom's status and legal guardianship. These courtroom proceedings would continue and escalate for almost the remainder of his life. As Sherman was approaching Georgia, General Bethune suddenly recognized the potential rights of Tom's parents, Mingo and Charity. The parents were coerced into signing an agreement that perpetuated Tom's servitude, giving Bethune 90 percent of Tom's earnings and keeping all control of Tom's services, paying his parents five hundred dollars a year and 10 percent of Tom's proceeds. In 1865, Tabbs Gross, an African-American promoter, acquired a one-half interest in Tom's management for twenty thousand dollars, leading to an unsuccessful custody battle between Gross and the Bethune family in a Cincinnati court. Custody ultimately remained with Bethune. In 1870, Tom was judged non compos mentis by a Virginia court and was committed to the care of General Bethune's son John. John soon married a divorcée, Eliza Stutzbach. When Tom and John returned from a lengthy tour, Eliza had filed for divorce. John Bethune was killed in a train accident in February of 1884, and his estate had been awarded entirely to his father, James; Eliza was cut out of his will. Eliza persuaded Tom's mother, Charity, to leave her home, rise up against her former master, and spearhead the campaign to gain legal custody and guardianship of Tom. Over the ensuing year, endless suits, appeals, and petitions in three separate states finally resulted in a victory that in May of 1887—twenty-two years after the end of the Civil War—finally led to freedom for Tom Wiggins or, as he was known by then, "the last American slave." [116] In subsequent promotional material, the court that had decided the matter was exaggerated, and Tom was advertised as "the last slave set free by order of the Supreme Court of the United States."[117]

As a musician and performer, Tom was electric, recalling the exaggerated, flamboyant playing of Liszt. His act was a carefully balanced mix of recital and variety show with classical pieces, popular hits, novelties, and audience participation; at his peak, he performed up to thirty-five concerts a month for nine months out of the year. Throughout his career, he toured the country extensively under several different management arrangements, earning approximately $20,000 a year, the equivalent of $5 million in today's dollars.[118] [119] By chance, Mark Twain encountered Tom on a train, wrote about him in a newspaper column, and became fascinated with Tom, never missing the opportunity to see him perform.[120] [121]Author Willa Cather also wrote a fictionalized account of an encounter with Tom.[122] Later in life, Tom became a regular on the vaudeville circuit. His compositions were eventually transcribed to capitalize on the growing demand for piano sheet music by young women who learned piano as a "sign of their refinement."[123]

Tom died in 1908. His burial site is in dispute: it is either Columbus, Georgia, or Brooklyn, New York. In 2000, pianist John Davis released a highly recommended CD, *John Davis Plays Blind Tom*, containing many of Tom's most popular and stirring compositions.

VIII

Blind Blues and Gospel Musicians

Terry Rowden introduces the reader to this genre of blind musicians with "if, as [legendary and deceased blues guitarist] B. B. King has declared, 'To be a blues singer is like having to be black twice,' then...being a blind blues singer was often like having to be black at least three times."[124] American blues came into being at the turn of the twentieth century, and during its growth period from approximately 1920 to 1945, the word *blind* became utilized as a professional appellation for a large number of sightless musicians.[125] [126] [127] Record companies would typically add the honorific title and not always in accordance with the artist's self-identification.[128] [129] Blind bluesmen (again, there were a paucity of female blind blues musicians) attempted to make a living in a relatively new musical genre in one of the few ways available to them.[130]

Fig. 14. Blind Lemon Jefferson. Date and photographer
unknown. Image courtesy of Jas Obrecht.

Blind Lemon Jefferson (1897–1929) (Fig 11), the foremost male blues performer of the 1920s, was the first prominent blues musician to be identified as blind on record labels and in advertisements.[131] He was born in Texas and was congenitally blind—etiology unknown. He developed a jazz-like improvisation and technically difficult guitar style that was probably influenced by Mexican flamenco guitarists[132] paired with high, clear, expressive vocals.[133] Some evidence suggests that Jefferson might have had residual light perception but no functional vision.[134] His first blues records were instant hits, and he is considered the undisputed father of Texas blues.[135] Accounts of his death are varied—he is said to have died when a driver abandoned him in a Chicago snowstorm or to have gotten lost and either suffered a heart attack or froze to death while walking home.[136] [137] Essential listening would include "See That My Grave is Kept Clean," "Match Box Blues," and "Jack O' Diamonds Blues."

Blind Willie Johnson (c. 1900–1949) was one of the most influential and best-selling of the early blues-influenced gospel singers. The etiology of his blindness was probably an alkali burn:

> When Willie was three or four years old, about 1905, his mother died and his father married again. About the time he was seven years old, his father caught his second wife with another man and beat her. To get even with Willie's father, she threw a pan of lye water in the little boy's face, blinding him.[138]

Little more is known of his life—there are no known interviews or autobiographies. He devoted himself exclusively to religious and gospel music, hymns, and folk spirituals.[139] His performances were described as emotional outpourings, with vibrato, growling, and often wordless moaning accompanied by the slide guitar, exemplified by his most well-known song, "Dark Was the Night—Cold Was the Ground." He was a fluid guitar player, especially when playing with a bottleneck slide. More than any other sacred singer of his era, Blind

Willie Johnson left a deep imprint that resonates with folk, blues, and gospel artists today.[140] Another recommended piece is "Let Your Light Shine on Me."

Blind Willie McTell (1901–1959) had an exceptionally long career for a blind blues performer. He was early blind from unknown causes, attended schools for the blind in three different states, and could read and write music in Braille. While not as commercially successful as Blind Lemon Jefferson during the 1920s, he received more recognition over a longer period of time than any other blind blues performer, particularly for his skills on the twelve-string guitar.[141] [142] [143] [144] He defied the stereotypes of blues musicians: he was not a womanizer and did not die young but was a working, resourceful, professional musician who never achieved a hit record.[145] Years later, his country blues would be "discovered" by young white audiences. Essential listening includes "Death Cell Blues," "Travelin' Blues," "Low Rider's Blues," "Mama Let Me Scoop for You," and "Statesboro Blues."

Blind Boy Fuller (1907–1941) was one of the best known and most influential of the bluesmen from the Southeast. Born Fulton Allen, he became blind at the age of twenty, approximately eight years before he began to record.[146] [147] His examination by a physician for a social security application (Fig. 12) constitutes the only example of a documented ophthalmologic examination of any of the figures profiled in this review. He recorded 130 titles, all of which were released in the six years before his premature death at age thirty-three. Essential listening includes "Step It Up and Go" and "Trucking My Blues Away."

Blind Blake (c. 1880–c. 1935) is considered one of the founders of East Coast blues, a style that emphasized elegant instrumental mastery.[148] He perfected finger-picking, ragtime guitar with syncopated bass lines, playing on the level of many jazz guitarists of his day.[149] Essential listening includes "Blind Arthur's Breakdown," "Diddie Wah Diddie," and "Southern Rag."

C. A. 2
Form PA-751
10-36

C O P Y

SOCIAL SECURITY BOARD

1465

PHYSICIAN'S REPORT ON EYE EXAMINATION

Application No. __24__

Applicant's name __Fulton Allen__   Sex __Male__ Race __Colored__

Address __805 Colfax St., Durham, North Carolina__
        (Street and number)   (Municipality)   (County)   (State)

Date of birth __July 10, 1907__   Age at onset of blindness: Right eye __21__ Left eye __21__

DIAGNOSIS: (If primary eye condition or etiological factor is not the same for both eyes, divide space and indicate each separately.)

Eye condition primarily responsible for blindness __Right eye: Phthisis bulbi.__

__Left eye: Papilloma of the cornea evidently following old perforating ulcer.__

Secondary conditions if any __None__

Etiological factor responsible for primary eye condition __Probably gonorrhea conjunctivitis.__

If there is a history of eye injury state type and date __None.__

Describe the appearance of eyes, including fundi __Right eye: fundi, phthisis bulbi, secondary__

__glaucoma. Left eye: as above.__

CENTRAL VISUAL ACUITY:

	WITHOUT GLASSES Distance (20 feet)	Near (14 inches)	WITH GLASSES Distance (20 feet)	Near (14 inches)
Right eye	Nil		Nil	
Left eye	Nil		Nil	

Use Snellen notations in recording visions as 20/200, 10/200, etc. Use AMA reading card in determining near vision.

PERIPHERAL VISION: (To be recorded where accepted as a factor in blindness on persons whose central vision is so great as to render them ineligible for aid to the blind in the State and who by rough test show a marked field defect.)

To be done on a standard perimeter with a radius of 13 inches and a white test object 6 mm in diameter. The test object should be of such size that it subtends an angle of approximately one degree.

Is there any limitation in the field of vision? _____ Right eye _____ Left eye _____

What is widest diameter in degrees of remaining visual field? _____ Right eye _____ Left eye _____

Prognosis (Is there any likelihood that vision could be restored by operation or treatment?) __Nil__

Recommendations—Primary eye condition __None.__

Recommendations—Etiological condition _____

Remarks (When should applicant be reexamined?) __None.__

Date of examination __Aug. 4, 1937__   __Banks Anderson__
                                        (Signature of eye physician)

Date of report __Aug. 4, 1937__   __McPherson Hospital__
                                        (Address)

Fig. 15. Physician examination of Fulton Allen (Blind Boy Fuller) for 1937 Social Security application. Image courtesy of Jas Obrecht.

Finally, two notable ensembles of blind musicians—the Blind Boys of Mississippi and the Blind Boys of Alabama—were popular in the 1950s and 1960s. Both groups were originally formed at state schools for the blind in their respective states. As gospel music transformed from the small local church to larger tent and arena gatherings, both of these groups became admired for their harmonies and adaptations of hymns and spirituals.[150] The Blind Boys of Alabama still actively record and perform.[151]

IX

Doc Watson (1923-2012)

Born in rural North Carolina, Arthel Watson lost vision before his first birthday, a case of early blindness and, as is typical of these stories, the cause is uncertain. Despite numerous interviews, he never spoke publicly about his blindness other than to reflect that God had given him his affliction to keep him humble. He intimated that perhaps contaminated sliver nitrate drops instilled after birth caused infections that rendered him blind. Medically speaking, that is highly unlikely, and no other external signs of infection of the eyelids or adnexae* were noted by his family.[152] With another biographer stating that his blindness was due to a "defect in the vessels that carry blood to the eye" with subsequent "infections,"[153] it is likely that all accounts are imprecise. He refused to wear the dark glasses commonly associated with blind performers, and many photographs reveal relatively intact globes with severe corneal scarring and leukoma in the left eye and some degree of corneal scarring in the right eye (Fig. 16). He acquired his nickname after achieving modest recognition early in his career, when the need for a short name suitable for radio led someone to suggest, "call him Doc."[154]

---

* Adnexae: accessory structures to the eye, including the eyelids, lashes, and lacrimal (tear) system.

Fig. 16. Doc Watson, country blues guitarist. Severe corneal scarring is seen in the left eye and possible mild scarring exists in the right eye. Photographer and date unknown.

As a child, Watson attended Raleigh School for the Blind, now the Governor Morehead School for the Blind, receiving music lessons in several instruments, composition, and notation. At the time, it was considered one of the finest schools for musical study, whether for sighted or blind children.[155] Two efforts to restore Watson's sight were unsuccessful: as a child, he was taken to a faith healer, and in 1962, he consulted with an ophthalmologist who told him that, at the age of forty, he was too old for a corneal transplant and would not benefit from it even if it were performed.* [156]

Watson learned and became adept at piano tuning at school, but he wanted to play bluegrass music and to play both guitar and banjo. Watson's father carved a banjo out of a maple tree and used a groundhog hide for the head. Unsatisfied with the tone of that head, his father ended up using the tanned hide of a recently deceased family cat for

---

* Corneal transplantation is now performed for patients of all ages.

the banjo head. Doc loved it and repeatedly claimed that "there was no sound quite like that banjo."[157] He started as a street performer, buying a series of guitars of ever-higher quality in attempts to refine the country twang tone that would become his signature sound.

Watson embraced his rural background and became skilled in flat-picking and fingerpicking guitar and banjo, playing and recording music from many different genres—folk, country, country blues, and rockabilly. His arrival on the music scene coincided perfectly with the rise of the steel string acoustic guitar as a lead instrument. He recorded and performed frequently with his son, Merle, before his son was killed in a tractor accident in 1985. Doc Watson was called a "national treasure" by President Jimmy Carter, was given the National Medal of the Arts by President Bill Clinton,[158] and won seven Grammy awards in several categories: country, folk, and ethnic/traditional.[159] Essential listening would be his early albums, *Doc Watson* and *Southbound.* Perhaps his best-known album, *Will the Circle Be Unbroken,* recorded with the Nitty Gritty Dirt Band and released in 1972, was a three-record platinum-selling recording that received two Grammy nominations. Particularly recommended are his songs "Deep River Blues" and "Shady Grove."

X

Art Tatum (1909-1956)

Art Tatum was born in Toledo, Ohio, and the etiology of his blindness is once again a matter of conjecture. He did not like to focus on his disability, and if questioned about it, he would often invent a story. Biographers have stated that cataract, diphtheria, measles, and scarlet fever were all possibilities, as were a football injury and a mugging incident.[160] Regardless of underlying cause, he had lost much of his vision by age four.[161] Because he maintained some degree of residual vision (Fig. 17)—he was estimated to have "one-eighth of normal vision"—he did not seek special considerations that were made available to the completely blind. That he should be regarded as one of the early pioneers of jazz is somewhat due to serendipity, as he was born in the same year as Benny Goodman, Lionel Hampton, and Gene Krupa.[162] Tatum went to a conservatory for two years, not a school for the blind.[163] Critics and peers alike have consistently applied the term genius to Tatum. Tatum's technical virtuosity on the piano and his extraordinary improvisational ability brought him praise from all parts of the jazz world.[164] He spent most of his career as a soloist, and essential recordings include his exquisite renditions of "Tea for Two," "Willow, Weep for Me," and "Someone to Watch Over Me."

Fig. 17. Portrait of Art Tatum, Vogue Room, New York, N.Y., between 1946 and 1948. Photograph by William P. Gottlieb. The left eye is probably phthisical and the right, although possibly turning slightly outward, appears to be looking at the camera.

XI

Ray Charles (1930–2004)

One of the twentieth century's most beloved musicians, Ray Charles was a sharecropper's son, born into poverty in rural Georgia. He began losing vision at age four and was totally blind by age seven. In his autobiography, *Brother Ray*,[165] he recalls being able to see colors and the slow process of losing vision. He saw three doctors, but no diagnosis or treatment was given or at least recollected. Because of the time course, symptoms, and eventual need for enucleation* of his right eye, it is widely believed—but not proven—that he suffered from congenital glaucoma. Charles attended a segregated school for the blind but started playing music even before he lost his sight—"I was born with music inside me."[166] As a young man, he admired the piano playing of Art Tatum, colorfully recalling, "later, when I got fairly good at piano, I knew that I couldn't even carry Art Tatum's shit bucket."[167]

Early in his career, like so many blues singers who had preceded him, he was actually advertised as "Blind Ray Charles."[168] In his first publicity photograph, a retouch artist painted sunglasses on his face—some found his eyeless visage distressing (Fig. 18)—and the iconic image of Ray Charles was born. He, more than any performer before him, made sunglasses a standard part of the blind performer's public persona.[169] Being a handsome man, he was well positioned to benefit from television at precisely the time when a telegenic appearance and image were becoming as important to an artist's success

---

* Surgical removal of the eye.

Fig. 18. Ray Charles, preparing for a performance at Carnegie Hall, May 1966. Rare photograph of Charles without his signature sunglasses shows anophthalmos of both eyes. Photograph by Bill Ray.

as his or her music. Again quoting Rowden, "As his fame grew, Ray Charles became one of the few black or blind performers given regular access to television...thereby to the normative and legitimizing gaze of mainstream white America."[170]

Record companies like Atlantic and Motown fostered shifting tastes in popular music toward rhythm and blues and gospel. Charles became a ground-breaking musician, bridging country, popular, gospel tradition, R&B, and African-American church music into unparalleled success across racial lines.[171] An early example is his landmark 1962 album *Modern Sounds in Country and Western Music*. He became the first and only black man to win a Grammy Award and have a number one *Billboard* pop chart hit with a country and western song, "I Can't Stop Loving You."[172] He had seven singles in *Billboard*'s top ten,[173] and he won seventeen Grammy awards in pop, R&B, and gospel.[174] He was the first and only artist with Grammy award–winning songs in six different decades (1950s through 2000s) and the first and only artist to have ten Grammys for covers—songs originally recorded by others. No other artist has four Grammys in this category; Charles has ten.[175] He received numerous honorary doctorate degrees and was awarded the Kennedy Center Honors in 1986 and a Lifetime Achievement Award by the National Academy of Recording Arts and Sciences.[176] Essential listening includes the aforementioned album; the songs "What I'd Say," "Hit the Road, Jack," and "Georgia on My Mind"; and his utterly unique rendition of "America the Beautiful."

XII

Ronnie Milsap (b. 1943)

Like Doc Watson, Ronnie Milsap is another prominent North Carolinian and former student of the Governor Morehead School for the Blind in Raleigh. Diagnosed with congenital glaucoma at the age of five months, he recounts in his biography that he had "'light vision' [possible light perception] in my left eye. I couldn't see forms…but I could detect light, very, very slightly, if I looked into direct sunlight."[177] He was taken to live with his grandmother until he was six years old, when he was taken to the Governor Morehead School. He recalls listening to country music and having an insatiable curiosity about how things worked, disassembling the family's radios and alarm clocks. He learned to read and write in Braille and began playing the piano at age six and seriously studying violin at age seven, eventually learning a dozen instruments. He considers the piano his primary instrument, in part because it is "a big instrument and easy for me to find (onstage)."[178]

Milsap recounts that, at age fourteen, following an assault at school, he fell and hit his left "light vision" eye, resulting in the eye being "loosened in its socket. The vein that was the organ's life support had been torn." His situation deteriorated, with severe pain and visits to doctors in Raleigh, who

> stuck needles into my injured eye and filled it with fluids they
> hoped would dissolve the blood clot. This went on for months…

The physicians struggled in vain to freeze the eye, they tried lancing it to break up the clot.[179]

Eventually this became and intractable problem for Milsap, leading to an enucleation:

> The procedure was performed inside the school infirmary... that's where I left my eye. I wasn't given a general anesthetic... they gave me a local, which consisted of poking needles into my useless eye, after first deadening my face with a shot into my temple. Then the light-vision [left] eye was removed.[180]

In 1980, Dr. Bruce Shields examined him for pain in his right eye. He describes the profound sadness he experienced at Shields's recommendation for enucleation, as he had to give up the hope that "through laser surgery or whatever, they could attach a new eye to the old optic nerve."[181] Despite what is one of the most detailed ocular histories in all of the artists previously examined, readers with ophthalmic knowledge will spot some significant improbabilities in Milsap's recalled diagnoses and treatments, again highlighting the difficulty of ascertaining accurate medical history from early childhood.

At first, Ronnie Milsap was musically interested in rock and roll and R&B, but he made a conscious switch to the country music genre, moving to Nashville. He ultimately recorded more than forty number one hits on the country music charts, as well as numerous crossover hits; won six Grammy awards; and achieved a high level of commercial success and mainstream recognition.[182] [183] Recommended listening includes "Smoky Mountain Rain," "I Wouldn't Have Missed It for the World," "Stranger in My House," and "There's No Getting Over Me." Milsap continues to record and perform regularly.

XIII

Jeff Healey (1966–2008)

Jeff Healey, a Canadian-born blind guitarist, died in 2008 from complications and metastases of osteosarcoma.* His constellation of remote tumors and blindness is perfectly compatible with his ocular history: he had bilateral familial retinoblastoma.† Born Brian Alan Moody, he was adopted by Bud and Yvonne Healey at three months of age, became Norman Jeff Healy, and shortly thereafter was diagnosed with retinoblastoma. At seven months old, one of his eyes was enucleated. Cryotherapy‡ was attempted on the fellow eye, but it was unsuccessful, and the other eye was removed when he was eleven months old.[184]

Healey learned echolocation and became adept at using it to play hide-and-seek. He would eventually become proficient at finding his way around a stage by snapping his fingers. He had a miniature piano at age two and by age three had received his first guitar. His father played Hawaiian guitar, which is played horizontally—similar to a pedal steel guitar. Healey was too small to hold the guitar, so he put it on his bed

---

* An aggressive malignant tumor of the bone, sometimes seen in conjunction with other cancers that have a genetic basis.

† A malignant tumor of the retinal cells occurring in children. Sporadic (nongenetic) retinoblastomas account for the majority of cases and affect one eye only. Familial or heritable retinoblastomas are in both eyes (bilateral), and because they have a genetic basis, patients are at risk for development of other, non-ocular cancers such as osteosarcoma.

‡ The use of intense freezing for treatment of malignancy or other ocular conditions.

horizontally and played it from the side of the bed. Eventually he would move the guitar to his lap, but he retained the unusual and technically more difficult horizontal playing position (Fig. 19), moving up and down the frets like a keyboard, rather than the vertical playing position of most guitarists.[185]

Fig. 19. Jeff Healey, exhibiting his unusual horizontal style of guitar playing. Photograph by Paul Bergen.

Healey was imitative and, not understanding that some recordings featured overdubbing, learned to mimic multiple lines of music at the same time. He taught himself to play guitar, piano, drums, trumpet, and trombone but rejected formal conservatory training. He started playing country music, was bored by it, and switched to the more challenging genre of jazz. As he matured, he began playing blues-based music, impressing even legendary blues guitarist Stevie Ray Vaughan. The Jeff Healey Band played mostly blues-based popular music, had a hit single, "Angel Eyes," and a platinum-selling debut album, *See The Light,* in 1988.[186] Healey also appeared in the 1989 film *Roadhouse*, starring Patrick Swayze. By 2000, he wanted to return to his jazz roots and recorded three jazz CDs.[187]

Healey refused to use his blindness as a promotional tactic, wanting "to be known as a great musician, not a blind musician." His peers, other pop-rock guitarists, regarded him as one of the greatest guitar players in the world.[188] In 2005, Jeff's son, Derek, was born. He, too, had familial retinoblastoma, but he received local treatment to the tumors—possibly laser or cryotherapy—and as of 2014 has both eyes "fully intact and… (with)…great vision."[189]

XIV

Andrea Bocelli (b. 1958)

Italian tenor Andrea Bocelli wrote his autobiography, *The Music of Silence,* [190] on a Braille typewriter—with no ghostwriter—using "Amos Bardi" as his third-person literary stand-in, allowing him more freedom to reveal details of his childhood and early years. Bocelli was born almost completely blind in the Tuscany region and was diagnosed with congenital glaucoma. He was seen by numerous doctors and specialists and underwent many surgical procedures in the attempt to save some of his eyesight. As a young child, he developed frequent pain, a known sequela of congenital glaucoma, along with buphthalmos (Fig. 20),* but the sound of music seemed to give him some relief and was able to calm him.[191]

Bocelli attended a boarding school for the blind, and at the time was "still able to see partially."[192] He learned Braille, excelled at arithmetic, and became noticed by his friends and teachers for his outstanding voice. He recalls that his first performance in first grade was met with "thunderous applause" and reflects—echoing Homer—"On the one hand, nature has taken something from him [*sic*]; on the other, it has given him something else."[193]

---

* Buphthalmos (Gr., "ox eye") is an abnormally enlarged eye, most commonly seen in children with congenital glaucoma, in which high pressure inside the eye causes the developing eye to enlarge.

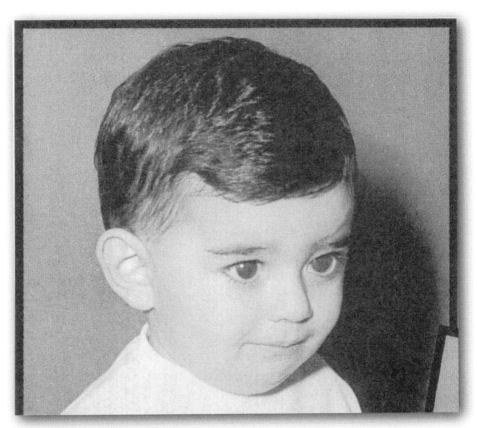

Fig. 20. Andrea Bocelli as a toddler. Buphthalmos (enlarged eye) and cloudy corneas are seen in both eyes. From Bocelli A. *The Music of Silence : A Memoir.* 1st US ed. New York, NY: Harper Entertainment; 2001. Photograph by Giovanni De Sandre. Used with permission.

In the fifth grade, he was playing soccer and was hit in the right eye, "the one that allowed him to see lights and colors." His limited vision began to dim, and he developed pain in the eye. He was taken to a hospital and was told that it was absolutely necessary to stop the hemorrhage caused by the impact of the ball. The doctor and nurse placed several leeches between the eye and temple of the little patient. They hoped that by sucking the blood, the leeches would help normalize the blood pressure within the eye.[194] By the time he was twelve, all remaining vision was gone.

Bocelli's voice garnered him early notice and praise. He began winning local competitions and attended the Cavazza Institute in Bologna, a regular high school with sighted students that also contained a music conservatory for blind students. He had a gift for learning languages, studied Greek and Latin, and began private study with a tutor who taught him languages, history, and literature. At a young age, he began playing piano, eventually finding work as a singer/pianist at a local piano bar. Bocelli also began taking courses and exams in preparation for a law degree. Serendipitously, a piano tuner who heard him sing suggested that he formally study singing. He began vocal lessons in Prato with Maestro Bettarini; learned about proper breathing, resonance, and vibrato; and became a serious vocal student.[195]

Bocelli would rise to international prominence, first by touring with Zucchero, a well-loved Italian artist, followed by an introduction to the legendary tenor Luciano Pavarotti,[196] then winning the newcomers category at the prestigious San Remo Festival in 1994.[197] His international popularity was propelled in 1996 by the release of one of his best-known songs, "Con Te Partirò," which topped charts and enjoyed enormous unit sales in many European countries.[198] In the same year, he performed the song as a duet with the English singer Sarah Brightman for a television special. "Time to Say Goodbye" became one of the best-selling singles of all time.[199] Bocelli has seven CDs that were in the *Billboard* top ten over the period from 1999 to 2013.[200] "Con Te Partirò," along with several collections of operatic arias, recorded operas in which he was the lead tenor, and special-themed or holiday CDs would be essential listening. Bocelli is a once-in-a-generation vocal talent whose appeal has extended across many genres.

XV

Stevie Wonder (b. 1950)

In Mark Riboswky's 2010 biography, Stevie Wonder is quoted, "Just because a man lacks the use of his eyes doesn't mean he lacks vision,"[201] effectively encapsulating the historical and musical significance of a truly imaginative and "amazing child prodigy whose talent appeared...from nowhere and...evolved into genius."[202] Born two months premature in Saginaw, Michigan, Stevland Hardaway Judkins, later Stevland Morris[203] had a birth weight of approximately four pounds and, as was the standard of care, received supplemental oxygen in an incubator, resulting in a blinding case of retinopathy of prematurity.* [204] In no available reference, however, is there mention of his visual acuity or status of the globes—phthisis, surgical anophthalmos, etc.

Wonder was given intensive musical training at the Michigan State School for the Blind; had a private tutor daily teaching him orchestra, piano, and voice; and learned to play string bass, violin, piano, harmonica, and drums. He studied music composition, chord structure, and classical music.[205] He was brought to the attention of

---

* Retinopathy of prematurity (ROP) is a condition seen only in premature babies who have undergone oxygen therapy in an incubator. The retinal blood vessels are still developing in these premature infants and, when exposed to high levels of oxygen (needed to support life in these critical patients with underdeveloped lungs), become damaged. Growth of new retinal blood vessels (neovascularization) occurs, resulting if untreated in hemorrhage in the eye, scar tissue formation, detachment of the retina, and ultimately blindness. Modern methods of carefully monitoring oxygen levels, screening premature infants, and revolutionary treatments have made ROP a rare condition in developed countries.

Motown Records founder, Berry Gordy Jr., who signed him with the label at the age of eleven. Various accounts exist regarding his name—that a conductor gave him the name "Wonder" at age twelve after hearing two of his concerts or that Gordy bestowed the name. His debut album, *Recorded Live: The Twelve-Year-Old Genius*, under the new moniker Little Stevie Wonder (Fig. 21) with its number one hit single "Fingertips, Part 2," made him an instant star in 1963.[206] [207] This led to television appearances, although Motown initially found it difficult to book Wonder on television due to his rocking, body swaying, and rapid head-turning mannerisms, sometimes referred to as "blindisms" (Fig 22).[208] [209] Blindisms are thought to be an involuntary attempt by the blind individual who is not receiving sufficient stimuli to self-stimulate.[210] These behaviors have been noted in other figures like Ray Charles and were exaggerated and parodied in Eddie Murphy's impersonations of Stevie Wonder.[211]

LITTLE STEVIE WONDER
Here you see little Stevie Wonder —13-year-old genius and star of the entertainment world from the U.S.A. Acclaimed currently in Europe as an outstanding discovery, little Stevie Wonder—rhythm and blues specialist—like so many other top stars throughout the world, plays a HOHNER Chromatic Harmonica.

ENQUIRE AT YOUR LOCAL MUSIC SHOP OR FOR LATEST HOHNER HARMONICA CATALOGUE—JUST OFF THE PRESS—WRITE TO:

HOHNER
11-13 FARRINGDON ROAD, LONDON, E.C.1

Fig. 21. Advertisement for Little Stevie Wonder playing Hohner chromatic harmonica, c. 1963.

In 1964, he dropped the "little" from his name and in the late 1960s through the 1970s began releasing a string of highly successful, musically important, and critically acclaimed records. Notable songs from this rich period include "My Cherie Amour," "Signed, Sealed, Delivered," and the entirety of his *Talking Book, Innervisions, Songs in the Key of Life,* and *Hotter Than July* albums. Other remarkable accomplishments included a personal role in lobbying for a national holiday for Reverend Dr. Martin Luther King Jr.'s birthday and his vigorous human rights campaign against South African apartheid in the 1980s.[212]

Fig. 22. Stevie Wonder, date and photographer unknown.

Two other matters regarding Wonder's blindness and ophthalmologic situation are worth noting. Musically, Perone has speculated

Wonder seems to be drawn to flat keys more than most pop songwriters. I believe this is directly attributable to (being) a keyboard player. As an unsighted keyboard player, Wonder may have found that the black keys of the piano/synthesizer keyboard provide a more reliable tactile reference than do the white keys. As a result, keys such as A-flat, D-flat, and E-flat would be more suitable to Wonder's keyboard technique.[213]

Unfortunately, no objective evidence exists that might confirm or refute this fascinating notion that Wonder's disability might have played a role in the selection of key signatures for his music.

Second, in 1999, Wonder announced his intent to be evaluated as a candidate for a retinal implant.[214] Although one report incorrectly identified Wonder as having retinitis pigmentosa,* [215] another correctly reported that he would not be a candidate for the procedure, which ultimately led to the development of the Argus II retinal prosthesis.† [216]

Accolades and awards have been showered on Stevie Wonder, including twenty-five top ten hits on various *Billboard* charts;[217] an Academy Award for best song ("I Just Called to Say I Love You");[218] twenty-two Grammy awards in R&B, pop, instrumental, and producer categories, including three album of the year awards;[219] a Grammy lifetime achievement award; induction into the Rock and Roll Hall of Fame in 1989; and Kennedy Center Honors in 1999.[220] Perone beautifully sums up the musicianship of Wonder, calling him

one of the first musicians to control every note of a song on a recording by writing music and lyrics, singing all the vocal lines, playing all the instruments, and producing the session…(he is)

---

* Retinitis pigmentosa (RP) is a degenerative, frequently hereditary condition of the retina, resulting in night blindness, severe constriction of peripheral vision, and in some cases, total blindness.

† The Argus II retinal prosthesis is a unique apparatus consisting of a retinal implant of an electrode array and video equipped "glasses" that transmit signals to the retinal implant, which then transmits the signals through the optic nerve to the brain. This results in returning extremely limited form vision and is only used in highly specific cases of RP in which there is absolutely no vision ("no light perception"—see appendix).

perhaps the most adaptable musician of his time, fully integrating rock, R&B, blues, pop, gospel, hip-hop, and jazz in recording after recording...(he is)...a composer without peer.[221]

Wonder's latest project was the critically acclaimed *Songs in The Key of Life* tour, in which he performed each song from that groundbreaking 1976 album.

XVI

Summary of Biographical Material

A number of common threads among the aforementioned artists stand out: an almost universal birth into poverty; congenital or early blindness; an extremely early interest in and aptitude for music that was encouraged by family, economic circumstances, or both; and rise to prodigious levels of talent in one or more facets of music—composition or instrumental or vocal performance. This led to public acceptance and frequently to commercial success, allowing each person to rise above his disability and become a major influence in his genre(s). Almost universal is the frequently incomplete and sometimes wildly inaccurate records of the precise ophthalmic conditions that led to their blindness. Because of poverty, absence of first-person recollection in infancy or early childhood, absence of records, lack of medical care, lack of medical knowledge, desire for privacy, or aspiration for mainstream acceptance, the transmission of important medical facts to the historical record is nearly impossible in all but a handful of cases. Nonetheless, there are possibly other commonalities to these extraordinary musical individuals. Using Stevie Wonder as a contemporary example and noting his exceptional abilities in musical composition, arrangement, lyric writing, as well as his effortless mastery of numerous difficult-to-play instruments, we can infer that the structure or wiring of a blind musician's brain might somehow differ from a sighted musician's. We now turn our attention to the neurological aspects of blind musicianship.

XVII

Neurological Underpinnings of Blind Musicians and Cross-Modal Plasticity

The remainder of this review will focus on what is known about music and the brain, how they interact, and how a blind individual might develop supranormal musical abilities. In his fascinating book, *Musicophilia: Tales of Music and the Brain*, neurologist Oliver Sacks states there is "no single center in the brain for music—at least twelve scattered networks are involved." Sacks notes that music is innate to all cultures and that humans seem "genetically susceptible to music." He quotes Charles Darwin, who was puzzled about the evolutionary origins of music: "As neither the enjoyment nor the capacity of producing musical notes are faculties of the least use to man...they must be ranked among the most mysterious with which he is endowed."[222] Jeff Healey's bassist, Joe Rockman, said of his gifted blind bandleader, "His ears didn't hear more because he was blind. But his brain did."[223] Some interesting neuroanatomic differences between the brains of musicians and nonmusicians exist. These include a larger corpus callosum and cerebellar volume[224] and larger motor, auditory, and visuospatial cortical areas[225] in the brains of musicians compared to those of nonmusicians.

Kupers and Ptito very thoroughly reviewed animal and human studies that show numerous specific differences between the brains of blind and sighted subjects with regard to anatomy, function, connectivity, and metabolic activity.[226] In an excellent review of the subject,

Frasnelli et al. attribute these differences to cross-modal plasticity, defined as

> the adaptive reorganization of neurons to integrate the function of a new sensory modality following the loss of another... (it may)...partially explain the extraordinary abilities observed in persons with sensory loss...increasing evidence points now to the extensive colonization of the occipital cortex (OC)—traditionally considered as visual—by non-visual inputs in blind individuals. A plethora of studies demonstrated task-dependent activation of the OC during auditory and tactile processing in early blind subjects.[227]

Compared to late blind (LB) or sighted controls, early blind (EB) individuals have been shown to have superior skills across a variety of auditory tasks, including sound localization,[228] [229] [230] [231] [232] [233] auditory processing,[234] [235] and central auditory skills.[236] Studies using functional imaging techniques—functional magnetic resonance imaging (fMRI) or positron emission tomography (PET) scanning—have supported the significant tendency of EB individuals to recruit other areas of the brain, notably the occipital areas,[*] in auditory tasks and processing (Fig. 23).[237] [238] [239] [240] [241] [242] Functional imaging studies during tactile tasks in blind subjects also demonstrate cross-modal activation of visual cortical areas.[243] [244] [245] Notably, Cohen et al. demonstrated that congenitally blind (CB) and EB subjects had activation in the occipital areas with Braille reading, whereas LB subjects—those who lost vision after age fourteen in this particular study—did not.

---

[*] The occipital lobes of the brain are located in the most posterior (toward the back) portion of the brain and are responsible for processing visual stimuli. Signals travel from the retina through the optic nerves, all the way into the posterior occipital lobes, where they are interpreted by the brain as the images we see.

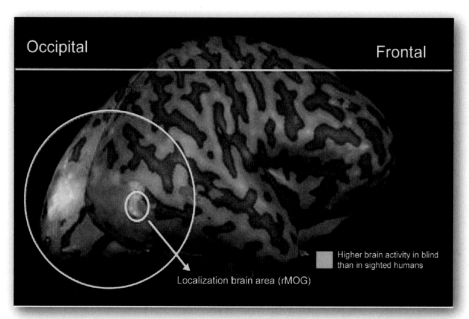

Fig. 23. Diagrammatic representation showing activated occipital areas of the brain that are higher in blind musicians than in sighted ones. Graphical abstract from Renier L, De Volder AG, Rauschecker JP. Cortical plasticity and preserved function in early blindness. *Neurosci Biobehav Rev.* 2014; 41: 53–63. Reprinted with permission, Elsevier, Ltd.

They concluded that "the development of…cross-modal plasticity in (the) visual cortex would seem to require the onset of blindness before adolescence, during a sensitive period of life" and that there seemed to be "a window of opportunity for…cross-modal plasticity in the blind."[246]

XVIII

Neuroplasticity with Amblyopia and Its Treatment as an Example

In an excellent recent review of the neural concepts underlying amblyopia,* Wong defines neuroplasticity as

> the dynamic ability of the brain to reorganize its connections functionally and structurally in responses to changes in the environment. The existence of critical periods in early postnatal life during which neuronal circuits display a heightened plasticity in response to external stimuli is well-established. After the end of the critical periods, plasticity declines dramatically.[247]

Amblyopia itself is an example of neuroplasticity, as optical or motor changes lead to abnormal signals that in turn lead to changes in cortical connections, suppressing the image from one eye or altering the mapping of the retina onto the visual cortex (abnormal retinal correspondence).[248]

The critical period for the development of binocularity† was traditionally thought to be the first seven to ten years of life.[249] Improved

---

* Amblyopia, frequently referred to as "lazy eye," is the inability of a non-diseased eye to see clearly. The result of a misalignment of the eye or a high refractive error like unilateral myopia (nearsightedness), the blurred or double image is suppressed by the growing child's brain and even if the misalignment or myopia is corrected later in life, the eye will not see clearly because, colloquially speaking, the eye did not "learn how to see."

† Two eyes working together in perfect conjunction producing fusion of images and resulting in depth perception.

visual acuity or performance after the so-called critical period in amblyopia has been demonstrated in numerous reports, offering additional examples of neuroplasticity. Older children treated for amblyopia demonstrated positive outcomes, with improved visual acuity in approximately 53 percent of patients.[250] [251]

Improvement in visual acuity has been noted in a series of adult patients with previously amblyopic eyes who lost vision due to age-related macular degeneration in their fellow eye.[252] Moreover, numerous studies have demonstrated improved visual acuity in adult amblyopes treated conventionally* [253] and improvement in visual acuity, Vernier acuity†, or visual functioning in adult amblyopes treated with perceptual learning techniques.[254] [255] [256] [257] [258] [259] [260] Levi concluded that "there is a good deal more plasticity in the adult sensory nervous system than previously suspected...when the somatosensory, auditory, or visual cortex is deprived of its normal sensory input, the area reorganizes."[261]

---

* Conventional treatment of amblyopia refers to patching the non-amblyopic "good" eye. More modern treatments of amblyopia include dilating eye drops and regimens other than occluding the sound eye.

† Vernier acuity refers to the highly precise level of visual acuity that humans have to detect any misalignment of two line segments. Finer resolution than Snellen (eye chart) visual acuity (see appendix).

XIX

Blind Musical Savants, Absolute Pitch, Neuroplasticity, and Possible Origins of Blind Musical Genius

In his absorbing book, Darold Treffert, a psychiatrist, advisor to the Academy Award–winning film *Rain Man,* and leading authority on the subject, defines savant syndrome as not a disease or disorder itself, but as a condition superimposed upon or coexistent with some other underlying condition, most frequently autistic disorder. Patients have an extraordinary ability, an "island of genius"—calendar calculating, musical ability, art, lightning calculating, or mechanical/spatial abilities—along with phenomenal memory. These special abilities tend to be associated with the right cerebral hemisphere and "coexist side by side, in jarring juxtaposition to certain disabilities" in logical, symbolic, and language skills associated with the left hemisphere. He postulates that this syndrome is most likely due to some form of pre- or immediate postnatal "left brain injury and right brain compensation...(and) facilitation of right brain capacities."[262]

As a subset, musical savants demonstrate certain common features: exceptional, frequently prodigious musical skills; poor verbal communication and social skills; a high incidence of absolute pitch; a "phonographic" memory; and, in a majority of cases, blindness.[263] [264] [265] [266] [267] The majority of musical savants are congenitally blind, usually due to one of three diseases: retinopathy of prematurity (ROP), septo-optic dysplasia (SOD),* or Leber's congenital amaurosis (LCA).† [268] Children with ROP and SOD are known to have high levels of musical interest and musical skills.[269] [270] Treffert reviews some of the earliest known or reported cases of blind musical savants, including a patient at the Salpêtrière French mental hospital in the 1830s[271] and Blind Tom Wiggins in the 1860s, then describes his personal work with Leslie Lemke. Leslie was born in 1952 with severe retinopathy of prematurity and profound mental retardation. A little-used piano had been in the house of the Lemke family since Leslie was seven. May Lemke, Leslie's adoptive mother, recalled for Treffert and in televised interviews that when Leslie was fourteen, the family was watching the movie *Sincerely Yours*, which featured Tchaikovsky's Piano Concerto No. 1. Late that night, Leslie's parents were awakened by the sound of Leslie perfectly playing the concerto from memory with no previous training whatsoever. Excellent video material is available demonstrating the extraordinary skills of Lemke and another prominent blind musical savant, Derek Paravicini.[272] [273] [274]

Lemke and Paravicini, like many blind autistic savants, have absolute pitch (AP). Sometimes referred to as perfect pitch, absolute pitch is the ability to immediately distinguish the pitch of any note without reference or comparison and to determine all the notes heard in a complex chord. More common in musicians, especially with early training,[275] it occurs only in about 10 percent of sighted musicians[276] and in 0.01 percent of the general population.[277] In contrast, approximately 50 to 60 percent of CB or EB children have absolute pitch,[278] [279] [280] as do 60 percent of blind musicians.[281] An unusually high percentage of children with ROP and SOD have, in addition to musical interest, absolute pitch.[282] [283] Two fMRI studies of absolute pitch show differences in activated areas between sighted musicians with AP and blind musicians with AP.[284] [285] Gaab et al. demonstrated that there was more activation in visual association areas during tone/pitch memory tasks performed

---

* A rare, congenital malformation in which there is underdevelopment of the optic nerve, pituitary gland underactivity, and malformation of the midline structures of the brain.

† A rare genetic disease of the retina with extremely poor vision dating from infancy.

by blind musicians with AP.[286] These data on AP lend further support to the neuroplastic changes that result in different neural networks in blind musicians than in sighted ones.

Acquired savant syndrome has also been reported in adult patients with frontotemporal dementia (FTD).* [287] [288] [289] In the largest series of sixty-nine patients with FTD, Miller et al. reported that, in the twelve patients with artistic or musical abilities, two demonstrated acquired musical abilities that were not present prior to their onset of FTD. They speculated that, since FTD causes unilateral left hemispheric degeneration (specifically, the left anterior temporal lobe), it could have led to "brain remodeling and consequent enhancement in function in the right hemisphere...parts necessary...for music and art."[290] A small number of congenital musical savants have undergone neuroimaging, confirming left hemispheric damage.[291] In savant syndrome, both congenital and acquired, there is strong evidence of neuroplastic changes with "recruitment of capacity from some other area of the brain or the release of dormant capacity in some other area of the brain."[292]

Renier et al. recently published a complete review of neuroplasticity in early blindness, and its graphical abstract available in the online version (Fig. 23) enhances our understanding of a complex process.[293] Ross et al. reported fMRI findings of a single CB musician with AP scanned while performing musical tasks. Similar to subjects in other studies, the subject demonstrated increased activation in visual association regions, possibly "recruiting them as accessory musical processing regions." The authors generalized that the possible genesis of supranormal musical abilities in CB and EB individuals might be similar to their case:

(our) subject...embodies the folkloric notion that because she is blind she has been able to develop superior musical abilities. Our

---

* Distinctly different from the more common Alzheimer's dementia, FTD is characterized by degeneration of brain cells in the front and side portions of the brain, resulting in characteristic changes in personality, behavior, movement, and speech.

data suggest a neurobiological basis for these reports. It is plausible that her remarkable musical aptitude may derive from the recruitment of visual cortical areas, thus allowing her to devote expanded neural networks to the performance of musical tasks.[294]

Merabet, reviewing mechanisms of neuroplasticity, agreed and expanded:

> There is direct experimental and clinical evidence that the recruitment of occipital areas is causally related to compensatory behaviors in the blind (and that)...the earlier the sensory loss, the more striking the neuroplastic effects...(leading some)...to suggest the existence of a precise critical period...beyond which functionally relevant cross-modal recruitment of occipital cortex...does not occur.[295]

The precise mechanism by which this occurs is unknown. Kypers and Ptito summarized the two leading theories of cross-modal plasticity in congenital blindness: cortical reorganization, in which new pathways are formed in the sensory deprived areas of the brain, and unmasking, in which loss of sensory input leads to consolidation of preexisting connections. Ultimately, they favored the unmasking hypothesis.[296] Sacks, too, discusses the dynamic activity in the brain with potentials that are normally suppressed or inhibited suddenly released by damage to other areas.[297] Musicality released by left hemispheric damage,[298] [299] [300] musical hallucinations released by deafness,[301] synesthesia* released by blindness,[302] [303] or visual hallucinations released by any damage along the visual pathway—Charles Bonnet syndrome† [304] [305] [306]—all constitute examples in which the delicate balance of excitatory and inhibitory forces is disrupted. Perhaps rewiring, recruitment, or release—or some

---

* Synesthesia (Gr., "joined or together perception"): Neurological phenomenon in which stimulation of one sensory mode elicits an automatic and involuntary response in another sensory area, e.g., hearing colors, seeing a color associated with a name or numeral.

† Condition in which severe visual loss (frequently age-related macular degeneration) leads to vivid visual hallucinations in patients without psychiatric illness.

combination—occurs in the deafferented[*] visual cortex of congenital or early blind musicians during the critical period[307] when the potential for neuroplasticity, as in amblyopes, is at its highest. This theoretical model, while well supported with a variety of data, provides evidence for a strong association yet still does not fully explain the causality of blind musicianship.

In conclusion, there appear to be several neurological pathways that potentially explain the genesis of prodigious musical talent in blind musicians. The brains of congenital or early blind musicians probably undergo extensive rewiring and recruitment of the dormant occipital (visual) cortex, adding auxiliary auditory and tactile processing centers that likely assist in the acquisition of skills needed to play a musical instrument. In contrast, blind musical savants probably have significant congenital left hemisphere damage, resulting in recruitment of right hemisphere functions. This rewiring, with possible release of inhibitory inputs, might enhance latent capacities in the right hemisphere associated with creativity, art, rhythm, and music.

---

[*] Loss of sensory input from one part of the body, in this case the visual input to the brain from non-functional eyes.

XX

Further Questions and Conclusions

In addition to the question of precise neurological underpinnings and genesis of musical talent in blind persons, other important and fascinating questions remain:

a) Have we seen a decrease in the number of cases of gifted blind musicians or geniuses? As our treatments have improved, almost all of the artists profiled would not have had the devastating visual outcome due to congenital glaucoma, retinopathy of prematurity, familial bilateral retinoblastoma, or cicatricial keratitis of various infectious etiologies. In the last half century, the decline in blinding disease in babies and young children has led to a decline in the number of blind musicians worldwide.[308] In his 2009 book, Rowden points out that "although [the relatively newer genre of] hip-hop is increasingly recognized...in...black popular culture, it is, tellingly, the only form of black popular music that has failed to sustain the career of a single blind or disabled performer."[309]

b) This leads to an intriguing hypothetical question: If these artists had been born in the present day, presumably treated or cured of their blinding conditions, would their musical gifts have been silenced or at least altered? With the compelling evidence that congenital or early blindness potentially sets the stage for increased auditory processing abilities, using the visual cortex for auxiliary areas of auditory and possible musical processing, the answer might be a tentative yes.

c) A variety of musical and sociological questions also remain. Where does mere aptitude end and serious or prodigious talent begin? What roles do limitation of opportunity or economic circumstance play in the development of auditory-based careers like music for blind individuals? Has race been a factor in the understanding, acceptance, or popularity of blind musicians? The reader is directed toward the fuller discussions available in the highly engaging books referenced, particularly those by Rowden,[310] Koestler,[311] O'Connell,[312] and Treffert.[313]

d) Finally, amblyopia treatment in older children and adults demonstrates that neuroplasticity can exist beyond the critical period early in life. In the sighted, neurologically intact musician, there is no substitute for practice and rehearsal, perhaps some good fortune, and a genetic predisposition to achieve musical skill. But further understanding of neuroplasticity in congenital and early blind musicians and in blind musical savants, acquired savant skills in frontotemporal dementia, and the interplay between excitatory and inhibitory areas raises this question: Could we someday develop modalities that would release, as Treffert puts it, "the inner savant that…resides, to some degree, within us all?"[314] Future research directed at the mechanisms of neuroplasticity and how they might be utilized to enhance potentials and abilities across a normal population is certainly warranted.

Finally, a philosophical coda: as musicians or music lovers, we can hope that new generations of musical geniuses will always be with us. As my fellow ophthalmologists and visual science researchers continue to expand the frontier of treatments for severe eye diseases, we hope to ensure these gifted artists will be drawn less and less often from the ranks of the blind.

Appendix: Visual Acuity Measurement

In common clinical practice of ophthalmology (or optometry), Snellen eye charts or some equivalent are used to measure vision. Specific-shaped letters ("optotypes") of smaller and smaller size are presented, and the patient is asked to read the smallest line. With best correction of spectacles or contact lenses or in a phoropter (a device that measures and corrects any refractive error), the patient's vision is recorded; 20/20 vision is considered normal distance vision. The top number signifies the test distance and the lower number the distance at which an optotype subtends five minutes of arc. Best corrected visual acuity of 20/200 is considered legally blind, and it is often incorrectly stated (although it helps with comprehension of the result) that the patient sees at two hundred feet what a person with 20/20 vision sees at twenty feet. Below are common Snellen acuities and implications. All acuities assume best possible refractive correction.

20/20	Normal visual acuity.
20/30	
20/40	Threshold for a driver's license in most states.
20/50	
20/60	
20/70	
20/80	
20/100	
20/200	Considered legally blind.
20/400	
Count Finger (CF)	Visual acuity worse than 20/400 is tested by the maximum distance at which the patient can count the examiner's fingers.
Hand Motions (HM)	Visual acuity worse than CF is tested by the maximum distance at which the patient can see the examiner's hand moving.
Light Perception (LP)	Visual acuity worse than HM is tested as the ability to see a bright light shined into the eye.
No Light Perception (NLP)	Complete blindness. Inability of the patient to see any light.

Notes

Notes to Introduction

1   Lusseyran J, Cameron ER. *And There Was Light: The Extraordinary Memoir of a Blind Hero of the French resistance in World War II.* 4th ed. Novato, New World Library; 2014.

2   Straus JN. *Extraordinary Measures: Disability in Music.* New York, NY: Oxford University Press; 2011.

3   Barasch M. *Blindness: The History of a Mental Image in Western Thought.* New York, NY: Routledge; 2001.

4   See note 3 above.

5   Rowden T. *The Songs of Blind Folk: African American Musicians and the Cultures of Blindness.* Ann Arbor, MI: University of Michigan Press; 2009.

6   Sacks OW. *Musicophilia: Tales of Music and the Brain.* Rev. and expanded 1st ed. New York, NY: Vintage Books; 2008.

7   See note 2 above.

8   See note 5 above.

Notes to Chapter 1

9   Koestler FA. *The Unseen Minority: A Social History of Blindness in America.* New York, NY: D. McKay; 1976.

Notes to Chapter 2

10   See note 2 above.

11   See note 5 above.

12   Lubet A. *Music, Disability, and Society.* Philadelphia, PA: Temple University Press; 2011.

13   Jimenez J, Olea J, Torres J, et al. Biography of Louis Braille and invention of the Braille alphabet. *Surv Ophthalmol.* 2009; 54(1): 142–9.

14   See note 12 above.

15   See note 2 above.

Notes to Chapter 3

16   French RS. *From Homer to Helen Keller: A Social and Educational Study of the Blind.* New York, NY: American Foundation for the Blind, Inc.; 1932.

17   See note 3 above.

18   See note 16 above.

19   Lang PH. *Music in Western Civilization.* New York, NY: W.W. Norton; 1997.

20   Graziosi B. *Inventing Homer: The Early Reception of the Epic.* Cambridge: Cambridge University Press; 2002.

21   See note 3 above.

22 See note 20 above.

23 See note 20 above.

24 See note 3 above.

25 See note 20 above.

26 See note 20 above.

27 Buxton RGA. *Myths and Tragedies in Their Ancient Greek Contexts.* 1st ed. Oxford: Oxford University Press; 2013.

28 See note 20 above.

Notes to Chapter 4

29 See note 2 above.

30 See note 19 above.

31 Balaban J. Blind Harry and "the Wallace." *The Chaucer Review.* 1974; 8(3): 214–51.

32 Hamilton W. *Blind Harry's Wallace.* Edinburgh: Luath Press; 1998.

33 See note 31 above.

34 Mackenzie JoG, Logan JFSA. *Sar-Obair nam Bard Gaelach: Or the Beauties of Gaelic Poetry and Lives of the Highland Bards.* Glasgow: MacGregor, Polson, & Co.; 1841.

35 See note 31 above.

36 See note 32 above.

37 Larrissy E. *The Blind and Blindness in Literature of the Romantic Period.* Edinburgh: Edinburgh University Press; 2007.

38 See note 6 above.

39 See note 37 above.

40 Gibson JG. *Traditional Gaelic Bagpiping 1745–1945.* Montreal: McGill-Queen's University Press; 1998.

41 See note 34 above.

42 See note 6 above.

43 See note 6 above.

44 Smallpox. World Health Organization website. http://www.who.int/csr/disease/smallpox/en/. Accessed August 10, 2015.

45 Semba RD. The ocular complications of smallpox and smallpox immunization. *Arch Ophthalmol.* 2003; 121(5): 715–9.

Notes to Chapter 5

46 Marmor MF. Vision loss and hearing loss in painting and musical composition. *Ophthalmology.* 2014; 121(7): 1480–5.

47 See note 2 above.

48 Gibbs K. Insights on Blindness and Composing. NewMusicBox website. http://www.newmusicbox.org/articles/insights-on-blindness-and-composing/. Posted Apr 14, 2010. Accessed August 10, 2015.

49   Learn about MIDI. MIDI Manufacturer's Association website. http://www.midi.org/aboutmidi/index.php. Accessed August 10, 2015.

50   See note 19 above.

51   See note 46 above.

52   Lang PH. *George Frideric Handel.* 1st ed. New York, NY: W. W. Norton; 1966.

53   Blanchard DL. George Handel and his blindness. *Doc Ophthalmol.* 1999; 99(3): 247–58.

54   Compositions by George Frideric Handel. Petrucci Music Library. International Music Score Library Project website. http://imslp.org/wiki/Category:Handel,_George_Frideric. Accessed August 14, 2015.

55   Hogwood C. *Handel.* Rev. ed. London: Thames & Hudson; 2007.

56   See note 53 above.

57   See note 53 above.

58   See note 55 above.

59   See note 46 above.

60   See note 52 above.

61   See note 55 above.

62   See note 53 above.

63   See note 55 above.

64 See note 52 above.

65 Albert DM, Henkind P. *Men of Vision: Lives of Notable Figures in Ophthalmology*. Philadelphia, PA: W. B. Saunders; 1993.

66 See note 52 above.

67 See note 65 above.

68 See note 65 above.

69 See note 55 above.

70 See note 53 above.

71 See note 2 above.

72 Calcraft, R. *Joaquin Rodrigo: Complete Biography*. Available from http://www.joaquin-rodrigo.com/index.php/en/biografia/10-autor/biografia/15-biografia-larga. Accessed August 14, 2015.

73 Kamhi de Rodrigo V. *Hand in Hand with Joaquín Rodrigo: My Life at the Maestro's Side*. Pittsburgh, PA: Latin American Literary Review Press, 1992.

74 See note 46 above.

75 See note 72 above.

76 Greenhaw E. *Diphtheria*. London: John W. Parker and Son; 1860.

77 Kingsford C. Diphtheria (letter). *The Lancet*. 1858; 72(1836): 484–6.

78 Stephenson S. Diphtheria of the conjunctiva. *The Lancet.* 1900; 155(3990): 451–2.

79 Moffatt SL, Cartwright VA, Stumpf TH. Centennial review of corneal transplantation. *Clin Experiment Ophthalmol.* 2005; 33(6): 642–57.

Notes to Chapter 6
80 See note 5 above.

81 Ramzy, CM. *A Musical Inheritance: Coptic Cantors and an Orally Transmitted Tradition.* From the Library of Congress. Available from http://www.loc.gov/item/ihas.200155645/#item-article. Accessed August 14, 2015.

82 Treffert DA. *Islands of Genius: The Bountiful Mind of the Autistic, Acquired, and Sudden Savant.* London: Jessica Kingsley; 2010.

83 Newlandsmith E. The Ancient Music of the Coptic Church. Lecture given at the University of Oxford May 21, 1931. Available from http://www.coptic.org/music/oxford.htm. Accessed July 4, 2015.

84 See note 81 above.

85 Kononenko NO: *Ukrainian Minstrels: And the Blind Shall Sing.* Armonk, NY: M. E. Sharpe; 1998.

86 See note 85 above.

87 See note 85 above.

88 Tradition and Tragedy: Ukraine's Kobzar Minstrels. Available from http://www.ukraine.com/blog/tradition-and-tragedy-ukraines-kobzar-minstrels. Accessed August 14, 2015.

89 See note 88 above.

90 See note 12 above.

91 El-Rashidi S. Egypt's blind women's orchestra struggles post-revolution. Available from http://www.al-monitor.com/pulse/originals/2014/05/egypt-blind-women-orchestra-nour-amal.html. Posted May 15, 2014. Accessed August 10, 2015.

92 See note 12 above.

93 See note 91 above.

Notes to Chapter 7

94 O'Connell D. *The Ballad of Blind Tom.* 1ˢᵗ ed. New York, NY: Overlook Duckworth; 2009.

95 See note 94 above.

96 O'Connell, D. Who was Blind Tom? Available from http://www.blind-tom.org/who_was_blind_tom.html. Accessed August 14, 2015.

97 See note 5 above.

98 See note 94 above.

99 See note 5 above.

100 Miller LK. *Musical Savants: Exceptional Skill in the Mentally Retarded.* Hillsdale, NJ: Erlbaum, 1989.

101 See note 94 above.

102 See note 94 above.

103 See note 94 above.

104 See note 5 above.

105 See note 94 above.

106 See note 5 above.

107 See note 2 above.

108 See note 94 above.

109 See note 2 above.

110 See note 2 above.

111 See note 82 above.

112 See note 94 above.

113 See note 5 above.

114 See note 94 above.

115 See note 5 above.

116 See note 94 above.

117 See note 5 above.

118 See note 94 above.

119 See note 96 above.

120 See note 94 above.

121 See note 2 above.

122 See note 5 above.

123 See note 94 above.

Notes to Chapter 8

124 See note 5 above.

125 Hansen B. *Rhino's Cruise through the Blues.* San Francisco, CA: Miller
     Freeman Books; 2000.

126 See note 5 above.

127 See note 6 above.

128 See note 5 above.

129 See note 6 above.

130 See note 5 above.

131 See note 5 above.

132 Vulcan Productions. The songs and the artists. PBS website. http://
www.pbs.org/theblues/songsartists/songsbioalpha.html. Accessed August 14, 2015.

133 Cohn L. *Nothing but the Blues: The Music and the Musicians*. New York,
NY: Abbeville Press; 1993.

134 See note 5 above.

135 See note 132 above.

136 See note 133 above.

137 See note 5 above.

138 Charters S. *The Country Blues*. New York, NY: Rinehart; 1959.

139 See note 5 above.

140 See note 133 above.

141 See note 133 above.

142 Komara EM. *Encyclopedia of the Blues*. New York, NY: Routledge, 2006.

143 See note 5 above.

144 Simkins T. Blind Willie McTell. Blind Willie McTell Blues Festival.
Available from http://www.blindwillie.com/about/blind-willie-
mctell/. Accessed August 10, 2015.

145 See note 142 above.

146 See note 12 above.

147 Herzhaft G, Harris P, Haussler J, Mikofsky AJ. *Encyclopedia of the Blues*. 2nd ed. Fayetteville, AR: University of Arkansas Press; 1997.

148 See note 147 above.

149 See note 5 above.

150 See note 5 above.

151 Home Page. Blind Boys of Alabama website. http://www.blindboys. com/. Accessed Aug 8, 2015.

Notes to Chapter 9

152 Gustavson K, Menius A, Tosic K. *Blind but Now I See: The Biography of Music Legend Doc Watson*. 2nd ed. New York, NY: Sumach Red Books; 2012.

153 Miller D. Doc Watson. *Flatpicking Guitar Magazine* 2(6). Available from http://www.flatpick.com/category_s/2226.htm. Accessed Aug 8, 2015.

154 See note 152 above.

155 See note 152 above.

156 See note 152 above.

157 See note 152 above.

158 See note 153 above.

159 Past Grammy Winners: Doc Watson. Grammy Awards website. https://www.grammy.com/nominees/search?artist=%22Doc+Watson %22&field_nominee_work_value=&year=All&genre=All. Accessed August 14, 2015.

Notes to Chapter 10

160 Lester J. *Too Marvelous for Words: The Life and Genius of Art Tatum.* New York, NY: Oxford University Press; 1994.

161 Jazz Profiles from NPR: Art Tatum. NPR website. http://www.npr.org/ programs/jazzprofiles/archive/tatum.html. Accessed July 4, 2015.

162 See note 5 above.

163 See note 160 above.

164 See note 5 above.

Notes to Chapter 11

165 Charles R, Ritz D. *Brother Ray: Ray Charles' Own Story.* New York, NY: Dial Press; 1978.

166 See note 165 above.

167 See note 165 above.

168 See note 5 above.

169 Lydon M. *Ray Charles: Man and Music.* New York, NY: Routledge; 2004.

170 See note 5 above.

171 See note 5 above.

172 The Ray Charles Foundation. Ray Charles: Achievement & Awards. Ray Charles website. http://www.raycharles.com/RC/RC-AchievementsAwards.html. Accessed June 30, 2015.

173 Ray Charles Chart History. *Billboard Magazine* website. http://www.billboard.com/artist/1490110/ray-charles/chart?sort=position&f=379. Accessed June 30, 2015.

174 Past Grammy Winners: Ray Charles. Grammy Awards website. https://www.grammy.com/nominees/search?artist=%22Ray+Charles%22&field_nominee_work_value=&year=All&genre=All. Accessed August 14, 2015.

175 See note 172 above.

176 See note 172 above.

Notes to Chapter 12

177 Milsap R, Carter T. *Almost Like a Song.* New York, NY: McGraw-Hill; 1990.

178 See note 177 above.

179 See note 177 above.

180 See note 177 above.

181 See note 177 above.

182 See note 5 above.

183 Ronnie Milsap website. https://www.ronniemilsap.com/. Accessed July 4, 2015.

Notes to Chapter 13

184 Watson C. *Out of Darkness: The Jeff Healey Story*. Toronto: Dundurn Press; 2010.

185 See note 184 above.

186 Jeff Healey website. http://jeffhealey.com/. Accessed June 29, 2015.

187 See note 184 above.

188 See note 184 above.

189 Bliss K. Daisy's eye cancer fund helps kids like Jeff Healey's son save sight. *Samaritan Magazine* website. http://www.samaritanmag.com/musicians/daisy%E2%80%99s-eye-cancer-fund-helps-kids-jeff-healey%E2%80%99s-son-save-sight. Posted October 16, 2014. Accessed July 4, 2015.

190 Bocelli A. *The Music of Silence: A Memoir*. 1st US ed. New York, NY: Harper Entertainment; 2001.

191 See note 190 above.

192 See note 190 above.

193 See note 190 above.

194 See note 190 above.

195 See note 190 above.

196 See note 190 above.

197 Andrea Bocelli website. http://www.andreabocelli.com/. Accessed June 30, 2015.

198 See note 197 above.

199 See note 197 above.

200 Andrea Bocelli Chart History. *Billboard Magazine* website. http://www.billboard.com/artist/279059/andrea-bocelli/chart?sort=position&f=305. Accessed June 30, 2015.

Notes to Chapter 15

201 Ribowsky M. *Signed, Sealed, and Delivered: The Soulful Journey of Stevie Wonder.* Hoboken, NJ: John Wiley & Sons; 2010.

202 See note 5 above.

203 Perone JE. *The Sound of Stevie Wonder: His Words and Music.* Westport, CT: Praeger; 2006.

204 See note 201 above.

205 See note 201 above.

206 See note 203 above.

207 See note 5 above.

208 Lowenfeld B. *Our Blind Children: Growing and Learning with Them.* 3rd ed. Springfield, IL: Charles C. Thomas; 1971.

209 See note 5 above.

210 See note 208 above.

211 See note 203 above.

212 See note 203 above.

213 See note 203 above.

214 See note 5 above.

215 Stevie Wonder hoping for experimental eye surgery. CNN website. http://www.cnn.com/1999/SHOWBIZ/Music/12/03/stevie.wonder/index.html?eref=sitesearch. Published December 3, 1999. Accessed July 5, 2015.

216 Tribune News Services. Eye procedure wouldn't aid Stevie Wonder, specialist says. *Chicago Tribune* website. http://articles.chicagotribune.com/1999-12-04/news/9912040158_1_eye-chip-karen-infeld-wilmer-eye-institute. Published December 4, 1999. Accessed July 5, 2015.

217 Stevie Wonder Chart History. *Billboard Magazine* website. http://www.billboard.com/artist/280720/stevie-wonder/chart?sort=position&f=379. Accessed June 30, 2015.

218 See note 5 above.

219 Past Grammy Winners: Stevie Wonder. Grammy Awards website.

https://www.grammy.com/nominees/search?artist=%22Stevie+Wond er%22&field_nominee_work_value=&year=All&genre=All. Accessed August 14, 2015.

220 See note 203 above.

221 See note 203 above.

Notes to Chapter 17

222 See note 6 above.

223 See note 184 above.

224 Schlaug G. The brain of musicians: a model for functional and structural adaptation. *Ann N Y Acad Sci.* 2001; 930: 281–99.

225 See note 6 above.

226 Kupers R, Ptito M. Insights from darkness: what the study of blindness has taught us about brain structure and function. *Prog Brain Res.* 2011; 192: 17–31.

227 Frasnelli J, Collignon O, Voss P, Lepore F. Crossmodal plasticity in sensory loss. *Prog Brain Res.* 2011; 191: 233–49.

228 Gougoux F, Zatorre RJ, Lassonde M, et al. A functional neuroimaging study of sound localization: visual cortex activity predicts performance in early-blind individuals. *PLoS Biol.* 2005; 3(2): e27.

229 Lessard N, Pare M, Lepore F, Lassonde M. Early-blind human subjects localize sound sources better than sighted subjects. *Nature.* 1998; 395(6699): 278–80.

230 Muchnik C, Efrati M, Nemeth E, et al. Central auditory skills in blind and sighted subjects. *Scand Audiol.* 1991; 20(1): 19–23.

231 Roder B, Teder-Salejarvi W, Sterr A, et al. Improved auditory spatial tuning in blind humans. *Nature.* 1999; 400(6740): 162–6.

232 Voss P, Gougoux F, Lassonde M, et al. A positron emission tomography study during auditory localization by late-onset blind individuals. *Neuroreport.* 2006; 17(4): 383-8.

233 Voss P, Gougoux F, Zatorre RJ, et al. Differential occipital responses in early- and late-blind individuals during a sound-source discrimination task. *Neuroimage.* 2008; 40(2): 746-58.

234 Starlinger I, Niemeyer, W. Do the blind hear better? Investigations on auditory processing in congenital or early acquired blindness. *Audiology.* 1981; 20: 503–9.

235 Wan CY, Wood AG, Reutens DC, Wilson SJ. Early but not late-blindness leads to enhanced auditory perception. *Neuropsychologia.* 2010; 48(1): 344–8.

236 See note 230 above.

237 See note 228 above.

238 Kujala T, Palva MJ, Salonen O, et al. The role of blind humans' visual cortex in auditory change detection. *Neurosci Lett.* 2005; 379(2): 127–31.

239 Poirier C CO, Scheiber C, DeVolder A. Auditory motion processing in early blind subjects (letter). *Cogn Process.* 2004; 5: 254–6.

240 Renier L, De Volder AG, Rauschecker JP. Cortical plasticity and pre-served function in early blindness. *Neurosci Biobehav Rev.* 2014; 41: 53–63.

241 See note 232 above.

242 See note 233 above.

243 Cohen LG, Weeks RA, Sadato N, et al. Period of susceptibility for cross-modal plasticity in the blind. *Ann Neurol.* 1999; 45(4): 451–60.

244 Sadato N, Pascual-Leone A, Grafman J, et al. Neural networks for Braille reading by the blind. *Brain.* 1998; 121: 1213–29.

245 Sadato N, Pascual-Leone A, Grafman J, et al. Activation of the pri-mary visual cortex by Braille reading in blind subjects. *Nature.* 1996; 380(6574): 526–8.

246 See note 243 above.

Notes to Chapter 18

247 Wong AM. New concepts concerning the neural mechanisms of amblyopia and their clinical implications. *Can J Ophthalmol.* 2012; 47(5): 399–409.

248 Daw NW. Mechanisms of plasticity in the visual cortex. The Friedenwald Lecture. *Invest Ophthalmol Vis Sci.* 1994; 35(13): 4168–79.

249 Polat U. Functional architecture of long-range perceptual interac-tions. *Spat Vis.* 1999; 12(2): 143–62.

250 Birnbaum MH, Koslowe K, Sanet R. Success in ambylopia therapy as a function of age: a literature survey. *Am J Optom Physiol Opt.* 1977; 54(5): 269–75.

251 Scheiman MM, Hertle RW, Beck RW, et al. Randomized trial of treatment of amblyopia in children aged 7 to 17 years. *Arch Ophthalmol.* 2005; 123(4): 437–47.

252 El Mallah MK, Chakravarthy U, Hart PM. Amblyopia: is visual loss permanent? *Br J Ophthalmol.* 2000; 84(9): 952–6.

253 Kishimoto F, Fujii C, Shira Y, et al. Outcome of conventional treatment for adult amblyopia. *Jpn J Ophthalmol.* 2014; 58(1): 26–32.

254 Fronius M, Cirina L, Cordey A, Ohrloff C. Visual improvement during psychophysical training in an adult amblyopic eye following visual loss in the contralateral eye. *Graefes Arch Clin Exp Ophthalmol.* 2005; 243(3): 278–80.

255 Levi DM, Polat U. Neural plasticity in adults with amblyopia. *Proc Natl Acad Sci USA.* 1996; 93(13): 6830–4.

256 Li J, Thompson B, Deng D, et al. Dichoptic training enables the adult amblyopic brain to learn. *Curr Biol.* 2013; 23(8): R308–9.

257 Polat U. Restoration of underdeveloped cortical functions: evidence from treatment of adult amblyopia. *Restor Neurol Neurosci.* 2008; 26(4–5): 413–24.

258 Polat U, Ma-Naim T, Belkin M, Sagi D. Improving vision in adult amblyopia by perceptual learning. *Proc Natl Acad Sci USA.* 2004; 101(17) :6692–7.

259 Levi DM, Polat U, Hu YS. Improvement in Vernier acuity in adults with amblyopia. Practice makes better. *Invest Ophthalmol Vis Sci.* 1997; 38(8): 1493–510.

260 Zhou Y, Huang C, Xu P, Tao L, Qiu Z, Li X, et al. Perceptual learning improves contrast sensitivity and visual acuity in adults with anisometropic amblyopia. *Vision Res.* 2006; 46(5): 739–50.

261 Levi DM. Perceptual learning in adults with amblyopia: a reevaluation of critical periods in human vision. *Dev Psychobiol.* 2005; 46(3): 222–32.

Notes to Chapter 19

262 See note 82 above.

263 Hermelin B, O'Connor N, Lee S. Musical inventiveness of five idiots-savants. *Psychol Med.* 1987; 17(3): 685–94;

264 See note 100 above.

265 Pring L, Woolf K, Tadic V. Melody and pitch processing in five musical savants with congenital blindness. *Perception.* 2008; 37(2): 290–307.

266 See note 6 above.

267 See note 82 above.

268 See note 82 above.

269 Matawa, C. Exploring the musicality of children and young people with retinopathy of prematurity. *Br J Vis Impairment.* 2009; 27(3): 252–62.

270 Pring L, Ockelford A. Children with septo-optic dysplasia—musical interests, abilities and provision: the results of a parental survey. *Br J of Vis Impairment.* 2005; 23(2): 58–66.

271 Tredgold AF. *Mental Deficiency (Amentia).* New York, NY: William Wood & Co; 1908.

272 Leslie Lemke: ABC's That's Incredible 1981. Available from https://www.youtube.com/watch?v=ZWtZA-ZmOAM. Accessed July 5, 2015.

273 Derek Paravicini and Adam Ockelford. In the key of genius. Available from https://www.ted.com/talks/derek_paravicini_and_adam_ockelford_in_the_key_of_genius?language=en. Filmed March 2013. Accessed July 5, 2015.

274 Treffert DA. Leslie Lemke: Videos. Available from https://www.wisconsinmedicalsociety.org/professional/savant-syndrome/profiles-and-videos/videos/leslie-lemke-videos/. Accessed July 5, 2015.

275 Moulton C. Perfect pitch reconsidered. *Clin Med.* 2014; 14(5): 517–9.

276 See note 6 above.

277 See note 100 above.

278 See note 6 above.

279 See note 82 above.

280 Welch G. Observations on the incidence of absolute pitch (AP) ability in the early blind. *Psychology of Music.* 1988; 16(1): 77–80.

281 See note 6 above.

282 See note 269 above.

283 See note 270 above.

284 Gaab N, Schulze K, Ozdemir E, Schlaug G. Neural correlates of absolute pitch differ between blind and sighted musicians. *Neuroreport.* 2006; 17(18): 1853–7.

285 Hamilton RH, Pascual-Leone A, Schlaug G. Absolute pitch in blind musicians. *Neuroreport.* 2004; 15(5): 803–6.

286 See note 284 above.

287 Miller BL, Boone K, Cummings JL, Read SL, Mishkin F. Functional correlates of musical and visual ability in frontotemporal dementia. *Br J Psychiatry.* 2000; 176: 458–63.

288 See note 6 above.

289 See note 82 above.

290 See note 287 above.

291 See note 82 above.

292 See note 82 above.

293 See note 240 above.

294 Ross DA, Olson IR, Gore JC. Cortical plasticity in an early blind musician: an fMRI study. *Magn Reson Imaging.* 2003; 21(7): 821–8.

295 Merabet LB, Pascual-Leone A. Neural reorganization following sensory loss: the opportunity of change. *Nat Rev Neurosci.* 2010; 11(1): 44–52.

296 Kupers R, Ptito M. Compensatory plasticity and cross-modal reorganization following early visual deprivation. *Neurosci Biobehav Rev.* 2014; 41: 36–52.

297 See note 6 above.

298 See note 287 above.

299 See note 6 above.

300 See note 82 above.

301 See note 6 above.

302 See note 6 above.

303 Safran AB, Sanda N. Color synesthesia. Insight into perception, emotion, and consciousness. *Curr Opin Neurol.* 2015; 28(1): 36–44.

304 Cogan DG. Visual hallucinations as release phenomena. *Albrecht Von Graefes Arch Klin Exp Ophthalmol.* 1973; 188(2): 139–50.

305 Menon GJ, Rahman I, Menon SJ, Dutton GN. Complex visual hallucinations in the visually impaired: the Charles Bonnet Syndrome. *Surv Ophthalmol.* 2003; 48(1): 58–72.

306 Schadlu AP, Schadlu R, Shepherd JB 3rd. Charles Bonnet syndrome: a review. *Curr Opin Ophthalmol.* 2009; 20(3): 219–22.

307 Rauschecker JP. Cortical plasticity and music. *Ann NY Acad Sci.* 2001; 930: 330–6.

Notes to Chapter 20

308 See note 5 above.

309 See note 5 above.

310 See note 5 above.

311 See note 9 above.

312 See note 94 above.

313 See note 82 above.

314 See note 82 above.